HE WALKED AMONG US

The life of Christ as seen
through the eyes of
Matthew, Mark, Luke and John

Thomas Nelson Publishers
Nashville

INTRODUCTION

The purpose of the Gospel writers was to introduce Jesus the Savior through their record of His life. Divine inspiration gave each writer the words needed to present his account of Jesus' life as He walked among us.

Today, however, such a variety of interpretations of the Good News has resulted in untold hundreds of forms of the Christian faith. The various phases of each interpretation seem to have created more division than unity. Thus, there seems to be a need for unification rather than a division among Christians over interpretations.

The Psalmist stressed unity in 133:1. "Behold, how good and how pleasant it is for brethren to dwell together in unity!"

Certainly when our Lord was with us He emphasized unity. "And if a house is divided against itself, that house cannot stand" (Mark 3:25). Jesus made it unquestionably clear that He desired unity in faith.

There is a great need to appreciate the beauty and to understand the unique messages of each of the four Gospel writers by studying them as they were separately written. In its own way, each Gospel contributes important elements to the whole, but new and fuller understanding results when we share a blended narrative of the great truths Jesus taught and the wonderful works He did as He walked among us.

As we pass from scene to scene in the life of our Lord, we are given the inspired insights of each of the writers in an enriched rendering of a "harmonized" Gospel in the same words used in each individual text.

The Gospel writer giving the fullest record of an event has been chosen for the main entry of that account. Material from the other Gospel writers gives additional information and strengthens the validity of each event. Each "voice" is identified by chapter and verse throughout the book and every event carries a number found in the contents. We cannot be sure of the exact historical sequence of all that the Gospels record, but our blended Gospel suggests a probable progression of the three and one-half years of Christ's public ministry.

The purpose of this edition is to provide inspiration as each reader meets the Master of the Gospels. It is not a critical analysis or scholarly work. The publishers of this volume desire that as you walk and talk with Jesus in the company of those inspired writers who introduce Him, you will experience that joy and transformation of life which comes from knowing Him, whom to know is life everlasting.

CONTENTS

JESUS VENTURES FROM GALILEE........... 92

BEFORE THE BIRTH
OF A SAVIOR

1. Luke Dedicates His Gospel

Lk 1:1-4 [1]Inasmuch as many have taken in hand to set in order a narrative of those things which have been fulfilled among us, [2]just as those who from the beginning were eyewitnesses and ministers of the word delivered them to us, [3]it seemed good to me also, having had perfect understanding of all things from the very first, to write to you an orderly account, most excellent Theophilus, [4]that you may know the certainty of those things in which you were instructed.

2. The Word Came First

Jn 1:1-5 [1]In the beginning was the Word, and the Word was with God, and the Word was God. [2]He was in the beginning with God. [3]All things were made through Him, and without Him nothing was made that was made. [4]In Him was life, and the life was the light of men. ⁵And the light shines in the darkness, and the darkness did not comprehend it.

Jn 1:9–13 ⁹That was the true Light which gives light to every man coming into the world.

¹⁰He was in the world, and the world was made through Him, and the world did not know Him. ¹¹He came to His own, and His own did not receive Him. ¹²But as many as received Him, to them He gave the right to become children of God, to those who believe in His name: ¹³who were born, not of blood, nor of the will of the flesh, nor of the will of man, but of God.

3. A Family Waits for the First Child

Matt 1:1–17 ¹The book of the genealogy of Jesus Christ, the Son of David, the Son of Abraham:

²Abraham begot Isaac, Isaac begot Jacob, and Jacob begot Judah and his brothers. ³Judah begot Perez and Zerah by Tamar, Perez begot Hezron, and Hezron begot Ram. ⁴Ram begot Amminadab, Amminadab begot Nahshon, and Nahshon begot Salmon. ⁵Salmon begot Boaz by Rahab, Boaz begot Obed by Ruth, Obed begot Jesse, ⁶and Jesse begot David the king.

David the king begot Solomon by her who had been the wife of Uriah. ⁷Solomon begot Rehoboam, Rehoboam begot Abijah, and Abijah begot Asa. ⁸Asa begot Jehoshaphat, Jehoshaphat begot Joram, and Joram begot Uzziah. ⁹Uzziah begot Jotham, Jotham begot Ahaz, and Ahaz begot Hezekiah. [10]Hezekiah begot Manasseh, Manasseh begot Amon, and Amon begot Josiah. [11]Josiah begot Jeconiah and his brothers about the time they were carried away to Babylon.

[12]And after they were brought to Babylon, Jeconiah begot Shealtiel, and Shealtiel begot Zerubbabel. [13]Zerubbabel begot Abiud, Abiud begot Eliakim, and Eliakim begot Azor. [14]Azor begot Zadok, Zadok begot Achim, and Achim begot Eliud. [15]Eliud begot Eleazar, Eleazar begot Matthan, and Matthan begot Jacob. [16]And Jacob begot Joseph the husband of Mary, of whom was born Jesus who is called Christ.

[17]So all the generations from Abraham to David are fourteen generations, from David until the captivity in Babylon are fourteen generations, and from the captivity in Babylon until the Christ are fourteen generations.

Lk 3:23–38 [23]Now Jesus Himself began His ministry at about thirty years of age, being (as was supposed) the son of Joseph, the son of Heli, [24]the son of Matthat, the son of Levi, the son of Melchi, the son of Janna, the son of Joseph, [25]the son of Mattathiah, the son of Amos, the son of Nahum, the son of Esli, the son of Naggai, [26]the son of Maath, the son of Mattathiah, the son of Semei, the son of Joseph, the son of Judah, [27]the son of Joannas, the son of Rhesa, the son of Zerubbabel, the son of Shealtiel, the son of Neri, [28]the son of Melchi, the son of Addi, the son of Cosam, the son of Elmodam, the son of Er, [29]the son of Jose, the son of Eliezer, the son of Jorim, the son of Matthat, the son of Levi, ³⁰the son of Simeon, the son of Judah, the son of Joseph, the son of Jonan, the son of Eliakim, ³¹the son of Melea, the son of Menan, the son of Mattathah, the son of Nathan, the son of David, ³²the son of Jesse, the son of Obed, the son of Boaz, the son of Salmon, the son of Nahshon, ³³the son of Amminadab, the son of Ram, the son of Hezron, the son of Perez, the son of Judah, ³⁴the son of Jacob, the son of Isaac, the son of Abraham, the son of Terah, the son of Nahor, ³⁵the son of Serug, the son of Reu, the son of Peleg, the son of Eber, the son of Shelah, ³⁶the son of Cainan, the son of Arphaxad, the son of Shem, the son of Noah, the son of Lamech, ³⁷the son of Methuselah, the son of Enoch, the son of Jared, the son of Mahalalel, the son of Cainan, ³⁸the son of Enosh, the son of Seth, the son of Adam, the son of God.

4. *Getting Ready for Jesus*

Lk 1:5-25 ⁵There was in the days of Herod, the king of Judea, a certain priest named Zacharias, of the division of Abijah. His wife was of the daughters of Aaron, and her name was Elizabeth. ⁶And they were both righteous before God, walking in all the commandments and ordinances of the Lord blameless. ⁷But they had no child, because Elizabeth was barren, and they were both well advanced in years.

⁸So it was, that while he was serving as priest

before God in the order of his division, [9]according to the custom of the priesthood, his lot fell to burn incense when he went into the temple of the Lord. [10]And the whole multitude of the people was praying outside at the hour of incense. [11]Then an angel of the Lord appeared to him, standing on the right side of the altar of incense. [12]And when Zacharias saw him, he was troubled, and fear fell upon him.

[13]But the angel said to him, "Do not be afraid, Zacharias, for your prayer is heard; and your wife Elizabeth will bear you a son, and you shall call his name John [14]And you will have joy and gladness, and many will rejoice at his birth. [15]For he will be great in the sight of the Lord, and shall drink neither wine nor strong drink. He will also be filled with the Holy Spirit, even from his mother's womb. [16]And he will turn many of the children of Israel to the Lord their God. [17]He will also go before Him in the spirit and power of Elijah, 'to turn the hearts of the fathers to the children,' and the disobedient to the wisdom of the just, to make ready a people prepared for the Lord."

[18]And Zacharias said to the angel, "How shall I know this? For I am an old man, and my wife is well advanced in years."

[19]And the angel answered and said to him, "I am Gabriel, who stands in the presence of God, and was sent to speak to you and bring you these glad tidings. [20]But behold, you will be mute and not

able to speak until the day these things take place, because you did not believe my words which will be fulfilled in their own time."

²¹And the people waited for Zacharias, and marveled that he lingered so long in the temple. ²²But when he came out, he could not speak to them; and they perceived that he had seen a vision in the temple, for he beckoned to them and remained speechless.

²³So it was, as soon as the days of his service were completed, that he departed to his own house. ²⁴Now after those days his wife Elizabeth conceived; and she hid herself five months, saying, ²⁵"Thus the Lord has dealt with me, in the days when He looked on me, to take away my reproach among people."

5. Mary Gets the Message

Lk 1:26-38 ²⁶Now in the sixth month the angel Gabriel was sent by God to a city of Galilee named Nazareth, ²⁷to a virgin betrothed to a man whose name was Joseph, of the house of David. The virgin's name was Mary. ²⁸And having come in, the angel said to her, "Rejoice, highly favored one, the Lord is with you; blessed are you among women!"

²⁹But when she saw him, she was troubled at his saying, and considered what manner of greeting this was. ³⁰Then the angel said to her, "Do not be afraid, Mary, for you have found favor with God. ³¹And behold, you will conceive in your

womb and bring forth a Son, and shall call His name JESUS. ³²He will be great, and will be called the Son of the Highest; and the Lord God will give Him the throne of His father David. ³³And He will reign over the house of Jacob forever, and of His kingdom there will be no end."

³⁴Then Mary said to the angel, "How can this be, since I do not know a man?"

³⁵And the angel answered and said to her, "The Holy Spirit will come upon you, and the power of the Highest will overshadow you; therefore, also, that Holy One who is to be born will be called the Son of God. ³⁶Now indeed, Elizabeth your relative has also conceived a son in her old age; and this is now the sixth month for her who was called barren. ³⁷For with God nothing will be impossible."

³⁸Then Mary said, "Behold the maidservant of the Lord! Let it be to me according to your word." And the angel departed from her.

6. Two Mothers Share Their Expectations

Lk 1:39-56 ³⁹Now Mary arose in those days and went into the hill country with haste, to a city of Judah, ⁴⁰and entered the house of Zacharias and greeted Elizabeth. ⁴¹And it happened, when Elizabeth heard the greeting of Mary, that the babe leaped in her womb; and Elizabeth was filled with the Holy Spirit. ⁴²Then she spoke out with a loud voice and said, "Blessed are you among women, and blessed is the fruit of your womb! ⁴³But why is this granted to me, that the mother of my Lord should come to me? ⁴⁴For indeed, as soon as the voice of your greeting sounded in my ears, the babe leaped in my womb for joy. ⁴⁵Blessed is she who believed, for there will be a fulfillment of those things which were told her from the Lord."

⁴⁶And Mary said:

"My soul magnifies the Lord,
⁴⁷ And my spirit has rejoiced in God my
        Savior.
⁴⁸ For He has regarded the lowly state of His
        maidservant;
    For behold, henceforth all generations will
        call me blessed.
⁴⁹ For He who is mighty has done great
        things for me,
    And holy is His name.
⁵⁰ And His mercy is on those who fear Him
    From generation to generation.
⁵¹ He has shown strength with His arm;
    He has scattered the proud in the
        imagination of their hearts.
⁵² He has put down the mighty from their
        thrones,
    And exalted the lowly.
⁵³ He has filled the hungry with good things,
    And the rich He has sent away empty.
⁵⁴ He has helped His servant Israel,
    In remembrance of His mercy,

⁵⁵ As He spoke to our fathers,
  To Abraham and to his seed forever."

⁵⁶ And Mary remained with her about three months, and returned to her house.

JOHN THE BAPTIST
AND JESUS MAKE
THEIR APPEARANCE

7. Jesus' Forerunner Arrives

Lk 1:57–79 ⁵⁷Now Elizabeth's full time came for her to be delivered, and she brought forth a son. ⁵⁸When her neighbors and relatives heard how the Lord had shown great mercy to her, they rejoiced with her.

⁵⁹So it was, on the eighth day, that they came to circumcise the child; and they would have called him by the name of his father, Zacharias. ⁶⁰His mother answered and said, "No; he shall be called John."

⁶¹But they said to her, "There is no one among your relatives who is called by this name." ⁶²So they made signs to his father—what he would have him called.

⁶³And he asked for a writing tablet, and wrote, saying, "His name is John." So they all marveled.

⁶⁴Immediately his mouth was opened and his tongue loosed, and he spoke, praising God. ⁶⁵Then fear came on all who dwelt around them; and all these sayings were discussed throughout all the hill country of Judea. ⁶⁶And all those who heard them kept them in their hearts, saying, "What kind of child will this be?" And the hand of the Lord was with him.

⁶⁷Now his father Zacharias was filled with the Holy Spirit, and prophesied, saying:

⁶⁸"Blessed is the Lord God of Israel,
　　For He has visited and redeemed His
　　　　people,
⁶⁹ And has raised up a horn of salvation for us
　　In the house of His servant David,
⁷⁰ As He spoke by the mouth of His holy
　　　　prophets,
　　Who have been since the world began,
⁷¹ That we should be saved from our
　　　　enemies
　　And from the hand of all who hate us,
⁷² To perform the mercy promised to our
　　　　fathers
　　And to remember His holy covenant,
⁷³ The oath which He swore to our father
　　　　Abraham:
⁷⁴ To grant us that we,
　　Being delivered from the hand of our
　　　　enemies,
　　Might serve Him without fear,

75 In holiness and righteousness before I Iim
    all the days of our life.

76 "And you, child, will be called the prophet
    of the Highest;
    For you will go before the face of the Lord
    to prepare His ways,
77 To give knowledge of salvation to His
    people
    By the remission of their sins,
78 Through the tender mercy of our God,
    With which the Dayspring from on high
    has visited us;
79 To give light to those who sit in darkness
    and the shadow of death,
    To guide our feet into the way of peace."

8. Joseph Learns the Truth

Matt 1:18–25 18Now the birth of Jesus Christ was as
follows: After His mother Mary was betrothed to
Joseph, before they came together, she was found
with child of the Holy Spirit. 19Then Joseph her
husband, being a just man, and not wanting to
make her a public example, was minded to put her
away secretly. 20But while he thought about these
things, behold, an angel of the Lord appeared to
him in a dream, saying, "Joseph, son of David, do
not be afraid to take to you Mary your wife, for that
which is conceived in her is of the Holy Spirit.
21And she will bring forth a Son, and you shall call

His name JESUS, for He will save His people from
their sins."

²²So all this was done that it might be fulfilled
which was spoken by the Lord through the
prophet, saying: ²³"Behold, the virgin shall be with
child, and bear a Son, and they shall call His name
Immanuel," which is translated, "God with us."

²⁴Then Joseph, being aroused from sleep, did
as the angel of the Lord commanded him and took
to him his wife, ²⁵and did not know her till she had
brought forth her firstborn Son. And he called His
name JESUS.

9. Arrival of the Savior

Lk 2:1-7 ¹And it came to pass in those days that a
decree went out from Caesar Augustus that all the
world should be registered. ²This census first took
place while Quirinius was governing Syria. ³So all
went to be registered, everyone to his own city.

⁴Joseph also went up from Galilee, out of the
city of Nazareth, into Judea, to the city of David,
which is called Bethlehem, because he was of the
house and lineage of David, ⁵to be registered with
Mary, his betrothed wife, who was with child. ⁶So
it was, that while they were there, the days were
completed for her to be delivered. ⁷And she
brought forth her firstborn Son, and wrapped
Him in swaddling cloths, and laid Him in a manger, because there was no room for them in the
inn.

Jn 1:14 ¹⁴And the Word became flesh and dwelt

among us, and we beheld His glory, the glory as of the only begotten of the Father, full of grace and truth.

10. *"Unto You Is Born This Day . . ."*

Lk 2:8–20 [8]Now there were in the same country shepherds living out in the fields, keeping watch over their flock by night. [9]And behold, an angel of the Lord stood before them, and the glory of the Lord shone around them, and they were greatly afraid. [10]Then the angel said to them, "Do not be afraid, for behold, I bring you good tidings of great joy which will be to all people. [11]For there is born to you this day in the city of David a Savior, who is Christ the Lord. [12]And this will be the sign to you: You will find a Babe wrapped in swaddling cloths, lying in a manger."

[13]And suddenly there was with the angel a multitude of the heavenly host praising God and saying:

[14]"Glory to God in the highest,
  And on earth peace, goodwill toward
      men!"

[15]So it was, when the angels had gone away from them into heaven, that the shepherds said to one another, "Let us now go to Bethlehem and see this thing that has come to pass, which the Lord has made known to us." [16]And they came with haste and found Mary and Joseph, and the Babe

lying in a manger. ¹⁷Now when they had seen Him, they made widely known the saying which was told them concerning this Child. ¹⁸And all those who heard it marveled at those things which were told them by the shepherds. ¹⁹But Mary kept all these things and pondered them in her heart. ²⁰Then the shepherds returned, glorifying and praising God for all the things that they had heard and seen, as it was told them.

11. Life Begins in a Stable

Lk 2:21-38 ²¹And when eight days were completed for the circumcision of the Child, His name was called JESUS, the name given by the angel before He was conceived in the womb.

²²Now when the days of her purification according to the law of Moses were completed, they brought Him to Jerusalem to present Him to the Lord ²³(as it is written in the law of the Lord, "Every male who opens the womb shall be called holy to the LORD"), ²⁴and to offer a sacrifice according to what is said in the law of the Lord, "A pair of turtledoves or two young pigeons."

²⁵And behold, there was a man in Jerusalem whose name was Simeon, and this man was just and devout, waiting for the Consolation of Israel, and the Holy Spirit was upon him. ²⁶And it had been revealed to him by the Holy Spirit that he would not see death before he had seen the Lord's Christ. ²⁷So he came by the Spirit into the temple. And when the parents brought in the Child Jesus,

to do for Him according to the custom of the law,
⁰⁰he took Him up in his arms and blessed God and
said:

²⁹"Lord, now You are letting Your servant
        depart in peace,
    According to Your word;
³⁰ For my eyes have seen Your salvation
³¹ Which You have prepared before the face
        of all peoples,
³² A light to bring revelation to the Gentiles,
    And the glory of Your people Israel."

³³And Joseph and His mother marveled at
those things which were spoken of Him. ³⁴Then
Simeon blessed them, and said to Mary His
mother, "Behold, this Child is destined for the fall
and rising of many in Israel, and for a sign which
will be spoken against ³⁵(yes, a sword will pierce
through your own soul also), that the thoughts of
many hearts may be revealed."
³⁶Now there was one, Anna, a prophetess, the
daughter of Phanuel, of the tribe of Asher. She was
of a great age, and had lived with a husband seven
years from her virginity; ³⁷and this woman was a
widow of about eighty-four years, who did not
depart from the temple, but served God with fast-
ings and prayers night and day. ³⁸And coming in
that instant she gave thanks to the Lord, and spoke
of Him to all those who looked for redemption in
Jerusalem.

12. Men of Wisdom Visit the Savior

Matt 2:1–12 ¹Now after Jesus was born in Bethlehem of Judea in the days of Herod the king,
behold, wise men from the East came to Jerusalem, ²saying, "Where is He who has been born
King of the Jews? For we have seen His star in the
East and have come to worship Him."

³When Herod the king heard this, he was troubled, and all Jerusalem with him. ⁴And when he
had gathered all the chief priests and scribes of the
people together, he inquired of them where the
Christ was to be born.

⁵So they said to him, "In Bethlehem of Judea,
for thus it is written by the prophet:

⁶ 'But you, Bethlehem, in the land of Judah,
   Are not the least among the rulers of
      Judah;
   For out of you shall come a Ruler
   Who will shepherd My people Israel.'"

⁷Then Herod, when he had secretly called the
wise men, determined from them what time the
star appeared. ⁸And he sent them to Bethlehem
and said, "Go and search carefully for the young
Child, and when you have found Him, bring back
word to me, that I may come and worship Him
also."

⁹When they heard the king, they departed; and
behold, the star which they had seen in the East

went before them, till it came and stood over where the young Child was. ¹⁰When they saw the star, they rejoiced with exceedingly great joy. ¹¹And when they had come into the house, they saw the young Child with Mary His mother, and fell down and worshiped Him. And when they had opened their treasures, they presented gifts to Him: gold, frankincense, and myrrh.

¹²Then, being divinely warned in a dream that they should not return to Herod, they departed for their own country another way.

13. Herod Wants to Kill

Matt 2:13–18 ¹³Now when they had departed, behold, an angel of the Lord appeared to Joseph in a dream, saying, "Arise, take the young Child and His mother, flee to Egypt, and stay there until I bring you word; for Herod will seek the young Child to destroy Him."

¹⁴When he arose, he took the young Child and His mother by night and departed for Egypt, ¹⁵and was there until the death of Herod, that it might be fulfilled which was spoken by the Lord through the prophet, saying, "Out of Egypt I called My Son."

¹⁶Then Herod, when he saw that he was deceived by the wise men, was exceedingly angry; and he sent forth and put to death all the male children who were in Bethlehem and in all its districts, from two years old and under, according to the time which he had determined from the wise

men. ¹⁷Then was fulfilled what was spoken by Jeremiah the prophet, saying:

> ¹⁸"A voice was heard in Ramah,
>   Lamentation, weeping, and great
>   mourning,
>   Rachel weeping for her children,
>   Refusing to be comforted,
>   Because they are no more."

14. Nazareth Provides a Home

Matt 2:19–23 ¹⁹Now when Herod was dead, behold, an angel of the Lord appeared in a dream to Joseph in Egypt, ²⁰saying, "Arise, take the young Child and His mother, and go to the land of Israel, for those who sought the young Child's life are dead." ²¹Then he arose, took the young Child and His mother, and came into the land of Israel.

²²But when he heard that Archelaus was reigning over Judea instead of his father Herod, he was afraid to go there. And being warned by God in a dream, he turned aside into the region of Galilee. ²³And he came and dwelt in a city called Nazareth, that it might be fulfilled which was spoken by the prophets, "He shall be called a Nazarene."

15. Simple Beginnings for John and Jesus

Lk 1:80 ⁸⁰So the child grew and became strong in spirit, and was in the deserts till the day of his manifestation to Israel.

Lk 2:40 ⁴⁰And the Child grew and became strong in spirit, filled with wisdom; and the grace of God was upon Him.

16. First Trip to Jerusalem

Lk 2:41-51 ⁴¹His parents went to Jerusalem every year at the Feast of the Passover. ⁴²And when He was twelve years old, they went up to Jerusalem according to the custom of the feast. ⁴³When they had finished the days, as they returned, the Boy Jesus lingered behind in Jerusalem. And Joseph and His mother did not know it; ⁴⁴but supposing Him to have been in the company, they went a day's journey, and sought Him among their relatives and acquaintances. ⁴⁵So when they did not find Him, they returned to Jerusalem, seeking Him. ⁴⁶Now so it was that after three days they found Him in the temple, sitting in the midst of the teachers, both listening to them and asking them questions. ⁴⁷And all who heard Him were astonished at His understanding and answers. ⁴⁸So when they saw Him, they were amazed; and His mother said to Him, "Son, why have You done this to us? Look, Your father and I have sought You anxiously."

⁴⁹And He said to them, "Why did you seek Me? Did you not know that I must be about My Father's business?" ⁵⁰But they did not understand the statement which He spoke to them.

⁵¹Then He went down with them and came to

Nazareth, and was subject to them, but His mother kept all these things in her heart.

17. Growth in Four Ways

Lk 2:52 [52] And Jesus increased in wisdom and stature, and in favor with God and men.

18. Preaching in the Wilderness

Lk 3:1-6 [1] Now in the fifteenth year of the reign of Tiberius Caesar, Pontius Pilate being governor of Judea, Herod being tetrarch of Galilee, his brother Philip tetrarch of Iturea and the region of Trachonitis, and Lysanias tetrarch of Abilene, [2] while Annas and Caiaphas were high priests, the word of God came to John the son of Zacharias in the wilderness. [3] And he went into all the region around the Jordan, preaching a baptism of repentance for the remission of sins, [4] as it is written in the book of the words of Isaiah the prophet, saying:

> "The voice of one crying in the wilderness:
> 'Prepare the way of the LORD;
> Make His paths straight.
> [5] Every valley shall be filled
> And every mountain and hill brought low;
> The crooked places shall be made straight
> And the rough ways smooth;
> [6] And all flesh shall see the salvation of
> God.'"

Jn 1:7 ⁷This man came for a witness, to bear witness of the Light, that all through him might believe.

Mk 1:6 ⁶Now John was clothed with camel's hair and with a leather belt around his waist, and he ate locusts and wild honey.

19. John's Popularity and Power

Matt 3:5–10 ⁵Then Jerusalem, all Judea, and all the region around the Jordan went out to him ⁶and were baptized by him in the Jordan, confessing their sins.

⁷But when he saw many of the Pharisees and Sadducees coming to his baptism, he said to them, "Brood of vipers! Who warned you to flee from the wrath to come? ⁸Therefore bear fruits worthy of repentance, ⁹and do not think to say to yourselves, 'We have Abraham as our father.' For I say to you that God is able to raise up children to Abraham from these stones. ¹⁰And even now the ax is laid to the root of the trees. Therefore every tree which does not bear good fruit is cut down and thrown into the fire."

Lk 3:10–14 ¹⁰So the people asked him, saying, "What shall we do then?"

¹¹He answered and said to them, "He who has two tunics, let him give to him who has none; and he who has food, let him do likewise."

¹²Then tax collectors also came to be baptized, and said to him, "Teacher, what shall we do?"

¹³And he said to them, "Collect no more than what is appointed for you."

¹⁴Likewise the soldiers asked him, saying, "And what shall we do?"

So he said to them, "Do not intimidate anyone or accuse falsely, and be content with your wages."

20. Jesus Recognized as the Christ

Lk 3:15-18 ¹⁵Now as the people were in expectation, and all reasoned in their hearts about John, whether he was the Christ or not, ¹⁶John answered, saying to all, "I indeed baptize you with water; but One mightier than I is coming, whose sandal strap I am not worthy to loose. He will baptize you with the Holy Spirit and fire. ¹⁷His winnowing fan is in His hand, and He will thoroughly clean out His threshing floor, and gather the wheat into His barn; but the chaff He will burn with unquenchable fire."

¹⁸And with many other exhortations he preached to the people.

21. A Jordan River Baptism

Matt 3:13-17 ¹³Then Jesus came from Galilee to John at the Jordan to be baptized by him. ¹⁴And John tried to prevent Him, saying, "I need to be baptized by You, and are You coming to me?"

¹⁵But Jesus answered and said to him, "Permit it to be so now, for thus it is fitting for us to fulfill all righteousness." Then he allowed Him.

¹⁶When He had been baptized, Jesus came up immediately from the water; and behold, the heavens were opened to Him, and He saw the Spirit of God descending like a dove and alighting upon Him. ¹⁷And suddenly a voice came from heaven, saying, "This is My beloved Son, in whom I am well pleased."

Lk 3:23 ²³Now Jesus Himself began His ministry at about thirty years of age, being (as was supposed) the son of Joseph, the son of Heli.

22. Satan's Plans Fail

Lk 4:1–13 ¹Then Jesus, being filled with the Holy Spirit, returned from the Jordan and was led by the Spirit into the wilderness, ²being tempted for forty days by the devil. And in those days He ate nothing, and afterward, when they had ended, He was hungry.

³And the devil said to Him, "If You are the Son of God, command this stone to become bread."

⁴But Jesus answered him, saying, "It is written, 'Man shall not live by bread alone, but by every word of God.'"

⁵Then the devil, taking Him up on a high mountain, showed Him all the kingdoms of the world in a moment of time. ⁶And the devil said to Him, "All this authority I will give You, and their glory; for this has been delivered to me, and I give it to whomever I wish. ⁷Therefore, if You will worship before me, all will be Yours."

⁸And Jesus answered and said to him, "Get

behind Me, Satan! For it is written, 'You shall worship the LORD your God, and Him only you shall serve.'"

⁹Then he brought Him to Jerusalem, set Him on the pinnacle of the temple, and said to Him, "If You are the Son of God, throw Yourself down from here. ¹⁰For it is written:

> 'He shall give His angels charge over you,
> To keep you,'

¹¹and,

> 'In their hands they shall bear you up,
> Lest you dash your foot against a stone.'"

¹²And Jesus answered and said to him, "It has been said, 'You shall not tempt the LORD your God.'"

¹³Now when the devil had ended every temptation, he departed from Him until an opportune time.

Matt 4:11b ¹¹And behold, angels came and ministered to Him.

23. Jewish Leaders Approach John

Jn 1:15 ¹⁵John bore witness of Him and cried out, saying, "This was He of whom I said, 'He who comes after me is preferred before me, for He was before me.'"

Jn 1:19–28 ¹⁹Now this is the testimony of John, when the Jews sent priests and Levites from Jerusalem to ask him, "Who are you?"

²⁰He confessed, and did not deny, but confessed, "I am not the Christ."

²¹And they asked him, "What then? Are you Elijah?"

He said, "I am not."

"Are you the Prophet?"

And he answered, "No."

²²Then they said to him, "Who are you, that we may give an answer to those who sent us? What do you say about yourself?"

²³He said: "I am

'The voice of one crying in the wilderness:
"Make straight the way of the LORD,"'

as the prophet Isaiah said."

²⁴Now those who were sent were from the Pharisees. ²⁵And they asked him, saying, "Why then do you baptize if you are not the Christ, nor Elijah, nor the Prophet?"

²⁶John answered them, saying, "I baptize with water, but there stands One among you whom you do not know. ²⁷It is He who, coming after me, is preferred before me, whose sandal strap I am not worthy to loose."

²⁸These things were done in Bethabara beyond the Jordan, where John was baptizing.

24. *John Identifies Promised Messiah*

Jn 1:29-34 [29]The next day John saw Jesus coming toward him, and said, "Behold! The Lamb of God who takes away the sin of the world! [30]This is He of whom I said, 'After me comes a Man who is preferred before me, for He was before me.' [31]I did not know Him; but that He should be revealed to Israel, therefore I came baptizing with water."

[32]And John bore witness, saying, "I saw the Spirit descending from heaven like a dove, and He remained upon Him. [33]I did not know Him, but He who sent me to baptize with water said to me, 'Upon whom you see the Spirit descending, and remaining on Him, this is He who baptizes with the Holy Spirit.' [34]And I have seen and testified that this is the Son of God."

25. *Jesus Selects Twelve Followers*

Jn 1:35-51 [35]Again, the next day, John stood with two of his disciples. [36]And looking at Jesus as He walked, he said, "Behold the Lamb of God!"

[37]The two disciples heard him speak, and they followed Jesus. [38]Then Jesus turned, and seeing them following, said to them, "What do you seek?"

They said to Him, "Rabbi" (which is to say, when translated, Teacher), "where are You staying?"

[39]He said to them, "Come and see." They came and saw where He was staying, and remained

with Him that day (now it was about the tenth hour).

⁴⁰One of the two who heard John speak, and followed Him, was Andrew, Simon Peter's brother. ⁴¹He first found his own brother Simon, and said to him, "We have found the Messiah" (which is translated, the Christ). ⁴²And he brought him to Jesus.

Now when Jesus looked at him, He said, "You are Simon the son of Jonah. You shall be called Cephas" (which is translated, A Stone).

⁴³The following day Jesus wanted to go to Galilee, and He found Philip and said to him, "Follow Me." ⁴⁴Now Philip was from Bethsaida, the city of Andrew and Peter. ⁴⁵Philip found Nathanael and said to him, "We have found Him of whom Moses in the law, and also the prophets, wrote —Jesus of Nazareth, the son of Joseph."

⁴⁶And Nathanael said to him, "Can anything good come out of Nazareth?"

Philip said to him, "Come and see."

⁴⁷Jesus saw Nathanael coming toward Him, and said of him, "Behold, an Israelite indeed, in whom is no deceit!"

⁴⁸Nathanael said to Him, "How do You know me?"

Jesus answered and said to him, "Before Philip called you, when you were under the fig tree, I saw you."

⁴⁹Nathanael answered and said to Him, "Rabbi, You are the Son of God! You are the King of Israel!"

⁵⁰Jesus answered and said to him, "Because I said to you, 'I saw you under the fig tree,' do you believe? You will see greater things than these." ⁵¹And He said to him, "Most assuredly, I say to you, hereafter you shall see heaven open, and the angels of God ascending and descending upon the Son of Man."

MINISTRY TO THE PEOPLE BEGINS

26. Jesus Enhances Wedding in Cana

Jn 2:1–11 [1]On the third day there was a wedding in Cana of Galilee, and the mother of Jesus was there. [2]Now both Jesus and His disciples were invited to the wedding. [3]And when they ran out of wine, the mother of Jesus said to Him, "They have no wine."

[4]Jesus said to her, "Woman, what does your concern have to do with Me? My hour has not yet come."

[5]His mother said to the servants, "Whatever He says to you, do it."

[6]Now there were set there six waterpots of stone, according to the manner of purification of the Jews, containing twenty or thirty gallons apiece. [7]Jesus said to them, "Fill the waterpots with water." And they filled them up to the brim. [8]And He said to them, "Draw some out now, and

take it to the master of the feast." And they took it. ⁹When the master of the feast had tasted the water that was made wine, and did not know where it came from (but the servants who had drawn the water knew), the master of the feast called the bridegroom. ¹⁰And he said to him, "Every man at the beginning sets out the good wine, and when the guests have well drunk, then the inferior. You have kept the good wine until now!"

¹¹This beginning of signs Jesus did in Cana of Galilee, and manifested His glory; and His disciples believed in Him.

Jn 2:12 ¹²After this He went down to Capernaum, He, His mother, His brothers, and His disciples; and they did not stay there many days.

27. Jesus Cleans a Dirty Temple

Jn 2:13–22 ¹³Now the Passover of the Jews was at hand, and Jesus went up to Jerusalem. ¹⁴And He found in the temple those who sold oxen and sheep and doves, and the money changers doing business. ¹⁵When He had made a whip of cords, He drove them all out of the temple, with the sheep and the oxen, and poured out the changers' money and overturned the tables. ¹⁶And He said to those who sold doves, "Take these things away! Do not make My Father's house a house of merchandise!" ¹⁷Then His disciples remembered that it was written, "Zeal for Your house has eaten Me up."

¹⁸So the Jews answered and said to Him,

"What sign do You show to us, since You do these things?"

19Jesus answered and said to them, "Destroy this temple, and in three days I will raise it up."

20Then the Jews said, "It has taken forty-six years to build this temple, and will You raise it up in three days?"

21But He was speaking of the temple of His body. 22Therefore, when He had risen from the dead, His disciples remembered that He had said this to them; and they believed the Scripture and the word which Jesus had said.

Jn 2:23-25 23Now when He was in Jerusalem at the Passover, during the feast, many believed in His name when they saw the signs which He did. 24But Jesus did not commit Himself to them, because He knew all men, 25and had no need that anyone should testify of man, for He knew what was in man.

28. Salvation Explained to a Night Visitor

Jn 3:1-21 1There was a man of the Pharisees named Nicodemus, a ruler of the Jews. 2This man came to Jesus by night and said to Him, "Rabbi, we know that You are a teacher come from God; for no one can do these signs that You do unless God is with him."

3Jesus answered and said to him, "Most assuredly, I say to you, unless one is born again, he cannot see the kingdom of God."

⁴Nicodemus said to Him, "How can a man be born when he is old? Can he enter a second time into his mother's womb and be born?"

⁵Jesus answered, "Most assuredly, I say to you, unless one is born of water and the Spirit, he cannot enter the kingdom of God. ⁶That which is born of the flesh is flesh, and that which is born of the Spirit is spirit. ⁷Do not marvel that I said to you, 'You must be born again.' ⁸The wind blows where it wishes, and you hear the sound of it, but cannot tell where it comes from and where it goes. So is everyone who is born of the Spirit."

⁹Nicodemus answered and said to Him, "How can these things be?"

¹⁰Jesus answered and said to him, "Are you the teacher of Israel, and do not know these things? ¹¹Most assuredly, I say to you, We speak what We know and testify what We have seen, and you do not receive Our witness. ¹²If I have told you earthly things and you do not believe, how will you believe if I tell you heavenly things? ¹³No one has ascended to heaven but He who came down from heaven, that is, the Son of Man who is in heaven. ¹⁴And as Moses lifted up the serpent in the wilderness, even so must the Son of Man be lifted up, ¹⁵that whoever believes in Him should not perish but have eternal life. ¹⁶For God so loved the world that He gave His only begotten Son, that whoever believes in Him should not perish but have everlasting life. ¹⁷For God did not send His Son into the world to

condemn the world, but that the world through Him might be saved.

[18] "He who believes in Him is not condemned; but he who does not believe is condemned already, because he has not believed in the name of the only begotten Son of God. [19] And this is the condemnation, that the light has come into the world, and men loved darkness rather than light, because their deeds were evil. [20] For everyone practicing evil hates the light and does not come to the light, lest his deeds should be exposed. [21] But he who does the truth comes to the light, that his deeds may be clearly seen, that they have been done in God."

29. John Exerts His True Colors

Jn 3:22–36 [22] After these things Jesus and His disciples came into the land of Judea, and there He remained with them and baptized. [23] Now John also was baptizing in Aenon near Salim, because there was much water there. And they came and were baptized. [24] For John had not yet been thrown into prison.

[25] Then there arose a dispute between some of John's disciples and the Jews about purification. [26] And they came to John and said to him, "Rabbi, He who was with you beyond the Jordan, to whom you have testified—behold, He is baptizing, and all are coming to Him!"

[27] John answered and said, "A man can receive nothing unless it has been given to him from heaven. [28] You yourselves bear me witness, that I

said, 'I am not the Christ,' but, 'I have been sent
before Him.' ²⁹He who has the bride is the bridegroom; but the friend of the bridegroom, who
stands and hears him, rejoices greatly because of
the bridegroom's voice. Therefore this joy of mine
is fulfilled. ³⁰He must increase, but I must decrease.
³¹He who comes from above is above all; he who is
of the earth is earthly and speaks of the earth. He
who comes from heaven is above all. ³²And what
He has seen and heard, that He testifies; and no
one receives His testimony. ³³He who has received
His testimony has certified that God is true. ³⁴For
He whom God has sent speaks the words of God,
for God does not give the Spirit by measure. ³⁵The
Father loves the Son, and has given all things into
His hand. ³⁶He who believes in the Son has everlasting life; and he who does not believe the Son
shall not see life, but the wrath of God abides on
him."

30. Herod Imprisons John the Baptist

Lk 3:19 ¹⁹But Herod the tetrarch, [was] rebuked
by [John] concerning Herodias, his brother Philip's
wife, and for all the evils which Herod had done.

Mk 6:17–20 ¹⁷For Herod himself had sent and laid
hold of John, and bound him in prison for the sake
of Herodias, his brother Philip's wife; for he had
married her. ¹⁸Because John had said to Herod, "It
is not lawful for you to have your brother's wife."

¹⁹Therefore Herodias held it against him and
wanted to kill him, but she could not; ²⁰for Herod

feared John, knowing that he was a just and holy man, and he protected him. And when he heard him, he did many things, and heard him gladly.

Jn 4:1-3 [1]Therefore, when the Lord knew that the Pharisees had heard that Jesus made and baptized more disciples than John [2](though Jesus Himself did not baptize, but His disciples), [3]He left Judea and departed again to Galilee.

Jn 4:44 [44]For Jesus Himself testified that a prophet has no honor in his own country.

31. Jesus Talks to the Woman at the Well

Jn 4:4-43 [4]But He needed to go through Samaria.

[5]So He came to a city of Samaria which is called Sychar, near the plot of ground that Jacob gave to his son Joseph. [6]Now Jacob's well was there. Jesus therefore, being wearied from His journey, sat thus by the well. It was about the sixth hour.

[7]A woman of Samaria came to draw water. Jesus said to her, "Give Me a drink." [8]For His disciples had gone away into the city to buy food.

[9]Then the woman of Samaria said to Him, "How is it that You, being a Jew, ask a drink from me, a Samaritan woman?" For Jews have no dealings with Samaritans.

[10]Jesus answered and said to her, "If you knew the gift of God, and who it is who says to you,

'Give Me a drink,' you would have asked Him, and He would have given you living water."

¹¹The woman said to Him, "Sir, You have nothing to draw with, and the well is deep. Where then do You get that living water? ¹²Are You greater than our father Jacob, who gave us the well, and drank from it himself, as well as his sons and his livestock?"

¹³Jesus answered and said to her, "Whoever drinks of this water will thirst again, ¹⁴but whoever drinks of the water that I shall give him will never thirst. But the water that I shall give him will become in him a fountain of water springing up into everlasting life."

¹⁵The woman said to Him, "Sir, give me this water, that I may not thirst, nor come here to draw."

¹⁶Jesus said to her, "Go, call your husband, and come here."

¹⁷The woman answered and said, "I have no husband."

Jesus said to her, "You have well said, 'I have no husband,' ¹⁸for you have had five husbands, and the one whom you now have is not your husband; in that you spoke truly."

¹⁹The woman said to Him, "Sir, I perceive that You are a prophet. ²⁰Our fathers worshiped on this mountain, and you Jews say that in Jerusalem is the place where one ought to worship."

²¹Jesus said to her, "Woman, believe Me, the hour is coming when you will neither on this

mountain, nor in Jerusalem, worship the Father.
²²You worship what you do not know; we know
what we worship, for salvation is of the Jews. ²³But
the hour is coming, and now is, when the true
worshipers will worship the Father in spirit and
truth; for the Father is seeking such to worship
Him. ²⁴God is Spirit, and those who worship Him
must worship in spirit and truth."

²⁵The woman said to Him, "I know that Messiah is coming" (who is called Christ). "When He
comes, He will tell us all things."

²⁶Jesus said to her, "I who speak to you am
He."

²⁷And at this point His disciples came, and they
marveled that He talked with a woman; yet no one
said, "What do You seek?" or, "Why are You talking with her?"

²⁸The woman then left her waterpot, went her
way into the city, and said to the men, ²⁹"Come,
see a Man who told me all things that I ever did.
Could this be the Christ?" ³⁰Then they went out of
the city and came to Him.

³¹In the meantime His disciples urged Him,
saying, "Rabbi, eat."

³²But He said to them, "I have food to eat of
which you do not know."

³³Therefore the disciples said to one another,
"Has anyone brought Him anything to eat?"

³⁴Jesus said to them, "My food is to do the will
of Him who sent Me, and to finish His work. ³⁵Do
you not say, 'There are still four months and then

comes the harvest'? Behold, I say to you, lift up your eyes and look at the fields, for they are already white for harvest! [36]And he who reaps receives wages, and gathers fruit for eternal life, that both he who sows and he who reaps may rejoice together. [37]For in this the saying is true: 'One sows and another reaps.' [38]I sent you to reap that for which you have not labored; others have labored, and you have entered into their labors."

[39]And many of the Samaritans of that city believed in Him because of the word of the woman who testified, "He told me all that I ever did." [40]So when the Samaritans had come to Him, they urged Him to stay with them; and He stayed there two days. [41]And many more believed because of His own word.

[42]Then they said to the woman, "Now we believe, not because of what you said, for we ourselves have heard Him and we know that this is indeed the Christ, the Savior of the world."

[43]Now after the two days He departed from there and went to Galilee.

A GOOD BEGINNING
IN GALILEE

32. Warm Reception Greets Jesus

Jn 4:45 ⁴⁵So when He came to Galilee, the Galileans received Him, having seen all the things He did in Jerusalem at the feast; for they also had gone to the feast.

Lk 4:14-15 ¹⁴Then Jesus returned in the power of the Spirit to Galilee, and news of Him went out through all the surrounding region. ¹⁵And He taught in their synagogues, being glorified by all.

Mk 1:15 ¹⁵And saying, "The time is fulfilled, and the kingdom of God is at hand. Repent, and believe in the gospel."

33. A Nobleman's Son Healed

Jn 4:46-54 ⁴⁶So Jesus came again to Cana of Galilee where He had made the water wine. And there was a certain nobleman whose son was sick at Capernaum. ⁴⁷When he heard that Jesus had come out of Judea into Galilee, he went to Him and implored Him to come down and heal his son, for he was at the point of death. ⁴⁸Then Jesus said to him, "Unless you people see signs and wonders, you will by no means believe."

⁴⁹The nobleman said to Him, "Sir, come down before my child dies!"

⁵⁰Jesus said to him, "Go your way; your son lives." So the man believed the word that Jesus spoke to him, and he went his way. ⁵¹And as he was now going down, his servants met him and told him, saying, "Your son lives!"

⁵²Then he inquired of them the hour when he got better. And they said to him, "Yesterday at the seventh hour the fever left him." ⁵³So the father knew that it was at the same hour in which Jesus said to him, "Your son lives." And he himself believed, and his whole household.

⁵⁴This again is the second sign Jesus did when He had come out of Judea into Galilee.

34. *Without Honor at Home*

Lk 4:16-30 ¹⁶So He came to Nazareth, where He had been brought up. And as His custom was, He went into the synagogue on the Sabbath day, and stood up to read. ¹⁷And He was handed the book of the prophet Isaiah. And when He had opened the book, He found the place where it was written:

¹⁸"The Spirit of the LORD is upon Me,
Because He has anointed Me

To preach the gospel to the poor;
I Ie has sent Me to heal the brokenhearted,
To proclaim liberty to the captives
And recovery of sight to the blind,
To set at liberty those who are oppressed;
19 To proclaim the acceptable year of the
LORD."

20Then He closed the book, and gave it back to the attendant and sat down. And the eyes of all who were in the synagogue were fixed on Him. 21And He began to say to them, "Today this Scripture is fulfilled in your hearing." 22So all bore witness to Him, and marveled at the gracious words which proceeded out of His mouth. And they said, "Is this not Joseph's son?"

23He said to them, "You will surely say this proverb to Me, 'Physician, heal yourself! Whatever we have heard done in Capernaum, do also here in Your country.'" 24Then He said, "Assuredly, I say to you, no prophet is accepted in his own country. 25But I tell you truly, many widows were in Israel in the days of Elijah, when the heaven was shut up three years and six months, and there was a great famine throughout all the land; 26but to none of them was Elijah sent except to Zarephath, in the region of Sidon, to a woman who was a widow. 27And many lepers were in Israel in the time of Elisha the prophet, and none of them was cleansed except Naaman the Syrian."

28So all those in the synagogue, when they

heard these things, were filled with wrath, ²⁹and rose up and thrust Him out of the city; and they led Him to the brow of the hill on which their city was built, that they might throw Him down over the cliff. ³⁰Then passing through the midst of them, He went His way.

35. Arrival in New Home

Matt 4:13–16 ¹³And leaving Nazareth, He came and dwelt in Capernaum, which is by the sea, in the regions of Zebulun and Naphtali, ¹⁴that it might be fulfilled which was spoken by Isaiah the prophet, saying:

¹⁵"The land of Zebulun and the land of
        Naphtali,
    By the way of the sea, beyond the Jordan,
    Galilee of the Gentiles:
¹⁶ The people who sat in darkness have seen
        a great light,
    And upon those who sat in the region and
        shadow of death
    Light has dawned."

36. Fishermen Pass the Test

Lk 5:1–11 ¹So it was, as the multitude pressed about Him to hear the word of God, that He stood by the Lake of Gennesaret, ²and saw two boats standing by the lake; but the fishermen had gone from them and were washing their nets. ³Then He got into one of the boats, which was Simon's, and asked him to put out a little from the land. And He sat down and taught the multitudes from the boat.

⁴When He had stopped speaking, He said to Simon, "Launch out into the deep and let down your nets for a catch."

⁵But Simon answered and said to Him, "Master, we have toiled all night and caught nothing; nevertheless at Your word I will let down the net." ⁶And when they had done this, they caught a great number of fish, and their net was breaking. ⁷So they signaled to their partners in the other boat to come and help them. And they came and filled both the boats, so that they began to sink. ⁸When Simon Peter saw it, he fell down at Jesus' knees, saying, "Depart from me, for I am a sinful man, O Lord!"

⁹For he and all who were with him were astonished at the catch of fish which they had taken; ¹⁰and so also were James and John, the sons of Zebedee, who were partners with Simon. And Jesus said to Simon, "Do not be afraid. From now on you will catch men." ¹¹So when they had brought their boats to land, they forsook all and followed Him.

Mk 1:16–20 ¹⁶And as He walked by the Sea of Galilee, He saw Simon and Andrew his brother casting a net into the sea; for they were fishermen. ¹⁷Then Jesus said to them, "Follow Me, and I will make you become fishers of men." ¹⁸They immediately left their nets and followed Him.

¹⁹When He had gone a little farther from there, He saw James the son of Zebedee, and John his brother, who also were in the boat mending their nets. ²⁰And immediately He called them, and they left their father Zebedee in the boat with the hired servants, and went after Him.

37. Some Sabbath Miracles of Jesus

Mk 1:21-34 ²¹Then they went into Capernaum, and immediately on the Sabbath He entered the synagogue and taught. ²²And they were astonished at His teaching, for He taught them as one having authority, and not as the scribes.

²³Now there was a man in their synagogue with an unclean spirit. And he cried out, ²⁴saying, "Let us alone! What have we to do with You, Jesus of Nazareth? Did You come to destroy us? I know who You are—the Holy One of God!"

²⁵But Jesus rebuked him, saying, "Be quiet, and come out of him!" ²⁶And when the unclean spirit had convulsed him and cried out with a loud voice, he came out of him. ²⁷Then they were all amazed, so that they questioned among themselves, saying, "What is this? What new doctrine is this? For with authority He commands even the unclean spirits, and they obey Him." ²⁸And immediately His fame spread throughout all the region around Galilee.

²⁹Now as soon as they had come out of the synagogue, they entered the house of Simon and Andrew, with James and John. ³⁰But Simon's wife's mother lay sick with a fever, and they told

Him about her at once. ³¹So He came and took her by the hand and lifted her up, and immediately the fever left her. And she served them.

³²At evening, when the sun had set, they brought to Him all who were sick and those who were demon-possessed. ³³And the whole city was gathered together at the door. ³⁴Then He healed many who were sick with various diseases, and cast out many demons; and He did not allow the demons to speak, because they knew Him.

Matt 8:17 ¹⁷That it might be fulfilled which was spoken by Isaiah the prophet, saying:

"He Himself took our infirmities
And bore our sicknesses."

38. Jesus: Tired but Determined

Mk 1:35–38 ³⁵Now in the morning, having risen a long while before daylight, He went out and departed to a solitary place; and there He prayed. ³⁶And Simon and those who were with Him searched for Him. ³⁷When they found Him, they said to Him, "Everyone is looking for You."

³⁸But He said to them, "Let us go into the next towns, that I may preach there also, because for this purpose I have come forth."

Lk 4:42–43 ⁴²Now when it was day, He departed and went into a deserted place. And the crowd sought Him and came to Him, and tried to keep Him from leaving them; ⁴³but He said to them, "I must preach the kingdom of God to the other cities also, because for this purpose I have been sent."

Matt 4:23–25 ²³And Jesus went about all Galilee, teaching in their synagogues, preaching the gospel of the kingdom, and healing all kinds of sickness and all kinds of disease among the people. ²⁴Then His fame went throughout all Syria; and they brought to Him all sick people who were afflicted with various diseases and torments, and those who were demon-possessed, epileptics, and paralytics; and He healed them. ²⁵Great multitudes followed Him—from Galilee, and from Decapolis, Jerusalem, Judea, and beyond the Jordan.

39. A Leper Receives the Cure

Lk 5:12 ¹²And it happened when He was in a certain city, that behold, a man who was full of leprosy saw Jesus; and he fell on his face and implored Him, saying, "Lord, if You are willing, You can make me clean."

Mk 1:41–45 ⁴¹Then Jesus, moved with compassion, stretched out His hand and touched him, and said to him, "I am willing; be cleansed." ⁴²As soon as He had spoken, immediately the leprosy left him, and he was cleansed. ⁴³And He strictly warned him and sent him away at once, ⁴⁴and said to him, "See that you say nothing to anyone; but go your way, show yourself to the priest, and offer for your cleansing those things which Moses commanded, as a testimony to them."

⁴⁵However, he went out and began to proclaim

it freely, and to spread the matter, so that Jesus could no longer openly enter the city, but was outside in deserted places; and they came to Him from every direction.

Lk 5:15-16 ¹⁵However, the report went around concerning Him all the more; and great multitudes came together to hear, and to be healed by Him of their infirmities. ¹⁶So He Himself often withdrew into the wilderness and prayed.

40. Jesus Heals and Forgives

Mk 2:1-2 ¹And again He entered Capernaum after some days, and it was heard that He was in the house. ²Immediately many gathered together, so that there was no longer room to receive them, not even near the door. And He preached the word to them.

Lk 5:17-26 ¹⁷Now it happened on a certain day, as He was teaching, that there were Pharisees and teachers of the law sitting by, who had come out of every town of Galilee, Judea, and Jerusalem. And the power of the Lord was present to heal them. ¹⁸Then behold, men brought on a bed a man who was paralyzed, whom they sought to bring in and lay before Him. ¹⁹And when they could not find how they might bring him in, because of the crowd, they went up on the housetop and let him down with his bed through the tiling into the midst before Jesus.

²⁰When He saw their faith, He said to him, "Man, your sins are forgiven you."

²¹And the scribes and the Pharisees began to reason, saying, "Who is this who speaks blasphemies? Who can forgive sins but God alone?"

²²But when Jesus perceived their thoughts, He answered and said to them, "Why are you reasoning in your hearts? ²³Which is easier, to say, 'Your sins are forgiven you,' or to say, 'Rise up and walk'? ²⁴But that you may know that the Son of Man has power on earth to forgive sins"—He said to the man who was paralyzed, "I say to you, arise, take up your bed, and go to your house."

²⁵Immediately he rose up before them, took up what he had been lying on, and departed to his own house, glorifying God. ²⁶And they were all amazed, and they glorified God and were filled with fear, saying, "We have seen strange things today!"

41. Matthew Celebrates His Call with Friends

Mk 2:13-22 ¹³Then He went out again by the sea; and all the multitude came to Him, and He taught them. ¹⁴As He passed by, He saw Levi the son of Alphaeus sitting at the tax office. And He said to him, "Follow Me." So he arose and followed Him.

¹⁵Now it happened, as He was dining in Levi's house, that many tax collectors and sinners also sat together with Jesus and His disciples; for there were many, and they followed Him. ¹⁶And when the scribes and Pharisees saw Him eating with the tax collectors and sinners, they said to His

disciples, "How is it that He eats and drinks with tax collectors and sinners?"

[17]When Jesus heard it, He said to them, "Those who are well have no need of a physician, but those who are sick. I did not come to call the righteous, but sinners, to repentance."

[18]The disciples of John and of the Pharisees were fasting. Then they came and said to Him, "Why do the disciples of John and of the Pharisees fast, but Your disciples do not fast?"

[19]And Jesus said to them, "Can the friends of the bridegroom fast while the bridegroom is with them? As long as they have the bridegroom with them they cannot fast. [20]But the days will come when the bridegroom will be taken away from them, and then they will fast in those days. [21]No one sews a piece of unshrunk cloth on an old garment; or else the new piece pulls away from the old, and the tear is made worse. [22]And no one puts new wine into old wineskins; or else the new wine bursts the wineskins, the wine is spilled, and the wineskins are ruined. But new wine must be put into new wineskins."

Lk 5:39 [39]"And no one, having drunk old wine, immediately desires new; for he says, 'The old is better.'"

42. Jerusalem: Site of Spectacular Healings

Jn 5:1–45 [1]After this there was a feast of the Jews, and Jesus went up to Jerusalem. [2]Now there is in

Jerusalem by the Sheep Gate a pool, which is called in Hebrew, Bethesda, having five porches. ³In these lay a great multitude of sick people, blind, lame, paralyzed, waiting for the moving of the water. ⁴For an angel went down at a certain time into the pool and stirred up the water; then whoever stepped in first, after the stirring of the water, was made well of whatever disease he had. ⁵Now a certain man was there who had an infirmity thirty-eight years. ⁶When Jesus saw him lying there, and knew that he already had been in that condition a long time, He said to him, "Do you want to be made well?"

⁷The sick man answered Him, "Sir, I have no man to put me into the pool when the water is stirred up; but while I am coming, another steps down before me."

⁸Jesus said to him, "Rise, take up your bed and walk." ⁹And immediately the man was made well, took up his bed, and walked.

And that day was the Sabbath. ¹⁰The Jews therefore said to him who was cured, "It is the Sabbath; it is not lawful for you to carry your bed."

¹¹He answered them, "He who made me well said to me, 'Take up your bed and walk.'"

¹²Then they asked him, "Who is the Man who said to you, 'Take up your bed and walk'?" ¹³But the one who was healed did not know who it was, for Jesus had withdrawn, a multitude being in that place. ¹⁴Afterward Jesus found him in the

temple, and said to him, "See, you have been made well. Sin no more, lest a worse thing come upon you."

¹⁵The man departed and told the Jews that it was Jesus who had made him well.

¹⁶For this reason the Jews persecuted Jesus, and sought to kill Him, because He had done these things on the Sabbath. ¹⁷But Jesus answered them, "My Father has been working until now, and I have been working."

¹⁸Therefore the Jews sought all the more to kill Him, because He not only broke the Sabbath, but also said that God was His Father, making Himself equal with God. ¹⁹Then Jesus answered and said to them, "Most assuredly, I say to you, the Son can do nothing of Himself, but what He sees the Father do; for whatever He does, the Son also does in like manner. ²⁰For the Father loves the Son, and shows Him all things that He Himself does; and He will show Him greater works than these, that you may marvel. ²¹For as the Father raises the dead and gives life to them, even so the Son gives life to whom He will. ²²For the Father judges no one, but has committed all judgment to the Son, ²³that all should honor the Son just as they honor the Father. He who does not honor the Son does not honor the Father who sent Him.

²⁴"Most assuredly, I say to you, he who hears My word and believes in Him who sent Me has everlasting life, and shall not come into judgment, but has passed from death into life. ²⁵Most

assuredly, I say to you, the hour is coming, and now is, when the dead will hear the voice of the Son of God; and those who hear will live. ²⁶For as the Father has life in Himself, so He has granted the Son to have life in Himself, ²⁷and has given Him authority to execute judgment also, because He is the Son of Man. ²⁸Do not marvel at this; for the hour is coming in which all who are in the graves will hear His voice ²⁹and come forth—those who have done good, to the resurrection of life, and those who have done evil, to the resurrection of condemnation. ³⁰I can of Myself do nothing. As I hear, I judge; and My judgment is righteous, because I do not seek My own will but the will of the Father who sent Me.

³¹"If I bear witness of Myself, My witness is not true. ³² There is another who bears witness of Me, and I know that the witness which He witnesses of Me is true. ³³You have sent to John, and he has borne witness to the truth. ³⁴Yet I do not receive testimony from man, but I say these things that you may be saved. ³⁵He was the burning and shining lamp, and you were willing for a time to rejoice in his light. ³⁶But I have a greater witness than John's; for the works which the Father has given Me to finish—the very works that I do—bear witness of Me, that the Father has sent Me. ³⁷And the Father Himself, who sent Me, has testified of Me. You have neither heard His voice at any time, nor seen His form. ³⁸But you do not have His word abiding in you, because whom He sent, Him you do not

believe. ³⁹You search the Scriptures, for in them you think you have eternal life; and these are they which testify of Me. ⁴⁰But you are not willing to come to Me that you may have life.

⁴¹"I do not receive honor from men. ⁴²But I know you, that you do not have the love of God in you. ⁴³I have come in My Father's name, and you do not receive Me; if another comes in his own name, him you will receive. ⁴⁴How can you believe, who receive honor from one another, and do not seek the honor that comes from the only God? ⁴⁵Do not think that I shall accuse you to the Father; there is one who accuses you—Moses, in whom you trust."

43. Jesus Declares Himself Lord of the Sabbath

Mk 2:23–28 ²³Now it happened that He went through the grainfields on the Sabbath; and as they went His disciples began to pluck the heads of grain. ²⁴And the Pharisees said to Him, "Look, why do they do what is not lawful on the Sabbath?"

²⁵But He said to them, "Have you never read what David did when he was in need and hungry, he and those with him: ²⁶how he went into the house of God in the days of Abiathar the high priest, and ate the showbread, which is not lawful to eat except for the priests, and also gave some to those who were with him?"

²⁷And He said to them, "The Sabbath was

made for man, and not man for the Sabbath. [28]Therefore the Son of Man is also Lord of the Sabbath."

44. Doing Good on Holy Days

Lk 6:6–7 [6]Now it happened on another Sabbath, also, that He entered the synagogue and taught. And a man was there whose right hand was withered. [7]So the scribes and Pharisees watched Him closely, whether He would heal on the Sabbath, that they might find an accusation against Him.

Matt 12:11–12 [11]Then He said to them, "What man is there among you who has one sheep, and if it falls into a pit on the Sabbath, will not lay hold of it and lift it out? [12]Of how much more value then is a man than a sheep? Therefore it is lawful to do good on the Sabbath."

Mk 3:3–5 [3]And He said to the man who had the withered hand, "Step forward." [4]Then He said to them, "Is it lawful on the Sabbath to do good or to do evil, to save life or to kill?" But they kept silent. [5]And when He had looked around at them with anger, being grieved by the hardness of their hearts, He said to the man, "Stretch out your hand." And he stretched it out, and his hand was restored as whole as the other.

Lk 6:11 [11]But they were filled with rage, and discussed with one another what they might do to Jesus.

Mk 3:7-11 [7]But Jesus withdrew with His disciples to the sea. And a great multitude from Galilee followed Him, and from Judea [8]and Jerusalem and Idumea and beyond the Jordan; and those from Tyre and Sidon, a great multitude, when they heard how many things He was doing, came to Him. [9]So He told His disciples that a small boat should be kept ready for Him because of the multitude, lest they should crush Him. [10]For He healed many, so that as many as had afflictions pressed about Him to touch Him. [11]And the unclean spirits, whenever they saw Him, fell down before Him and cried out, saying, "You are the Son of God."

Matt 12:16-21 [16]Yet He warned them not to make Him known, [17]that it might be fulfilled which was spoken by Isaiah the prophet, saying:

[18]"Behold! My Servant whom I have chosen,
   My Beloved in whom My soul is well
      pleased!
   I will put My Spirit upon Him,
   And He will declare justice to the Gentiles.
[19] He will not quarrel nor cry out,
   Nor will anyone hear His voice in the
      streets.
[20] A bruised reed He will not break,
   And smoking flax He will not quench,
   Till He sends forth justice to victory;
[21] And in His name Gentiles will trust."

46. Jesus Needs Twelve Helpers

Lk 6:12-13 ¹²Now it came to pass in those days that He went out to the mountain to pray, and continued all night in prayer to God. ¹³And when it was day, He called His disciples to Himself; and from them He chose twelve whom He also named apostles.

Mk 3:14-19 ¹⁴Then He appointed twelve, that they might be with Him and that He might send them out to preach, ¹⁵and to have power to heal sicknesses and to cast out demons: ¹⁶Simon, to whom He gave the name Peter; ¹⁷James the son of Zebedee and John the brother of James, to whom He gave the name Boanerges, that is, "Sons of Thunder"; ¹⁸Andrew, Philip, Bartholomew, Matthew, Thomas, James the son of Alphaeus, Thaddaeus, Simon the Cananite; ¹⁹and Judas Iscariot, who also betrayed Him. And they went into a house.

47. Sermon Preached from a Mountaintop

Lk 6:17-19 ¹⁷And He came down with them and stood on a level place with a crowd of His disciples and a great multitude of people from all Judea and Jerusalem, and from the seacoast of Tyre and Sidon, who came to hear Him and be healed of their diseases, ¹⁸as well as those who were tormented with unclean spirits. And they were healed. ¹⁹And the whole multitude sought to touch Him, for power went out from Him and healed them all.

Matt 5:1-48 [1]And seeing the multitudes, He went up on a mountain, and when He was seated His disciples came to Him. [2]Then He opened His mouth and taught them, saying:

[3] "Blessed are the poor in spirit,
>For theirs is the kingdom of heaven.
[4] Blessed are those who mourn,
>For they shall be comforted.
[5] Blessed are the meek,
>For they shall inherit the earth.
[6] Blessed are those who hunger and thirst
>for righteousness,
>For they shall be filled.
[7] Blessed are the merciful,
>For they shall obtain mercy.
[8] Blessed are the pure in heart,
>For they shall see God.
[9] Blessed are the peacemakers,
>For they shall be called sons of God.
[10] Blessed are those who are persecuted for
>righteousness' sake,
>For theirs is the kingdom of heaven.

[11]"Blessed are you when they revile and persecute you, and say all kinds of evil against you falsely for My sake. [12]Rejoice and be exceedingly glad, for great is your reward in heaven, for so they persecuted the prophets who were before you.

[13]"You are the salt of the earth; but if the salt loses its flavor, how shall it be seasoned? It is then

good for nothing but to be thrown out and trampled underfoot by men.

14 "You are the light of the world. A city that is set on a hill cannot be hidden. 15 Nor do they light a lamp and put it under a basket, but on a lampstand, and it gives light to all who are in the house. 16 Let your light so shine before men, that they may see your good works and glorify your Father in heaven.

17 "Do not think that I came to destroy the Law or the Prophets. I did not come to destroy but to fulfill. 18 For assuredly, I say to you, till heaven and earth pass away, one jot or one tittle will by no means pass from the law till all is fulfilled. 19 Whoever therefore breaks one of the least of these commandments, and teaches men so, shall be called least in the kingdom of heaven; but whoever does and teaches them, he shall be called great in the kingdom of heaven. 20 For I say to you, that unless your righteousness exceeds the righteousness of the scribes and Pharisees, you will by no means enter the kingdom of heaven.

21 "You have heard that it was said to those of old, 'You shall not murder, and whoever murders will be in danger of the judgment.' 22 But I say to you that whoever is angry with his brother without a cause shall be in danger of the judgment. And whoever says to his brother, 'Raca!' shall be in danger of the council. But whoever says, 'You fool!' shall be in danger of hell fire. 23 Therefore if you bring your gift to the altar, and there remember that your brother has something against you,

²⁴leave your gift there before the altar, and go your way. First be reconciled to your brother, and then come and offer your gift. ²⁵Agree with your adversary quickly, while you are on the way with him, lest your adversary deliver you to the judge, the judge hand you over to the officer, and you be thrown into prison. ²⁶Assuredly, I say to you, you will by no means get out of there till you have paid the last penny.

²⁷"You have heard that it was said to those of old, 'You shall not commit adultery.' ²⁸But I say to you that whoever looks at a woman to lust for her has already committed adultery with her in his heart. ²⁹If your right eye causes you to sin, pluck it out and cast it from you; for it is more profitable for you that one of your members perish, than for your whole body to be cast into hell. ³⁰And if your right hand causes you to sin, cut it off and cast it from you; for it is more profitable for you that one of your members perish, than for your whole body to be cast into hell.

³¹"Furthermore it has been said, 'Whoever divorces his wife, let him give her a certificate of divorce.' ³²But I say to you that whoever divorces his wife for any reason except sexual immorality causes her to commit adultery; and whoever marries a woman who is divorced commits adultery.

³³"Again you have heard that it was said to those of old, 'You shall not swear falsely, but shall perform your oaths to the Lord.' ³⁴But I say to you, do not swear at all: neither by heaven, for it is

God's throne; ³⁵nor by the earth, for it is His footstool; nor by Jerusalem, for it is the city of the great King. ³⁶Nor shall you swear by your head, because you cannot make one hair white or black. ³⁷But let your 'Yes' be 'Yes,' and your 'No,' 'No.' For whatever is more than these is from the evil one.

³⁸"You have heard that it was said, 'An eye for an eye and a tooth for a tooth.' ³⁹But I tell you not to resist an evil person. But whoever slaps you on your right cheek, turn the other to him also. ⁴⁰If anyone wants to sue you and take away your tunic, let him have your cloak also. ⁴¹And whoever compels you to go one mile, go with him two. ⁴²Give to him who asks you, and from him who wants to borrow from you do not turn away.

⁴³"You have heard that it was said, 'You shall love your neighbor and hate your enemy.' ⁴⁴But I say to you, love your enemies, bless those who curse you, do good to those who hate you, and pray for those who spitefully use you and persecute you, ⁴⁵that you may be sons of your Father in heaven; for He makes His sun rise on the evil and on the good, and sends rain on the just and on the unjust. ⁴⁶For if you love those who love you, what reward have you? Do not even the tax collectors do the same? ⁴⁷And if you greet your brethren only, what do you do more than others? Do not even the tax collectors do so? ⁴⁸Therefore you shall be perfect, just as your Father in heaven is perfect."

Matt 6:1-31 [1] "Take heed that you do not do your charitable deeds before men, to be seen by them. Otherwise you have no reward from your Father in heaven. [2]Therefore, when you do a charitable deed, do not sound a trumpet before you as the hypocrites do in the synagogues and in the streets, that they may have glory from men. Assuredly, I say to you, they have their reward. [3]But when you do a charitable deed, do not let your left hand know what your right hand is doing, [4]that your charitable deed may be in secret; and your Father who sees in secret will Himself reward you openly.

[5]"And when you pray, you shall not be like the hypocrites. For they love to pray standing in the synagogues and on the corners of the streets, that they may be seen by men. Assuredly, I say to you, they have their reward. [6]But you, when you pray, go into your room, and when you have shut your door, pray to your Father who is in the secret place; and your Father who sees in secret will reward you openly. [7]And when you pray, do not use vain repetitions as the heathen do. For they think that they will be heard for their many words.

[8]"Therefore do not be like them. For your Father knows the things you have need of before you ask Him. [9]In this manner, therefore, pray:

Our Father in heaven,
Hallowed be Your name.

¹⁰ Your kingdom come.
Your will be done
On earth as it is in heaven.
¹¹ Give us this day our daily bread.
¹² And forgive us our debts,
As we forgive our debtors.
¹³ And do not lead us into temptation,
But deliver us from the evil one.
For Yours is the kingdom and the power
and the glory forever. Amen.

¹⁴"For if you forgive men their trespasses, your heavenly Father will also forgive you. ¹⁵But if you do not forgive men their trespasses, neither will your Father forgive your trespasses.

¹⁶"Moreover, when you fast, do not be like the hypocrites, with a sad countenance. For they disfigure their faces that they may appear to men to be fasting. Assuredly, I say to you, they have their reward. ¹⁷But you, when you fast, anoint your head and wash your face, ¹⁸so that you do not appear to men to be fasting, but to your Father who is in the secret place; and your Father who sees in secret will reward you openly.

¹⁹"Do not lay up for yourselves treasures on earth, where moth and rust destroy and where thieves break in and steal; ²⁰but lay up for yourselves treasures in heaven, where neither moth nor rust destroys and where thieves do not break in and steal. ²¹For where your treasure is, there your heart will be also.

²²"The lamp of the body is the eye. If therefore your eye is good, your whole body will be full of light. ²³But if your eye is bad, your whole body will be full of darkness. If therefore the light that is in you is darkness, how great is that darkness!

²⁴"No one can serve two masters; for either he will hate the one and love the other, or else he will be loyal to the one and despise the other. You cannot serve God and mammon.

²⁵"Therefore I say to you, do not worry about your life, what you will eat or what you will drink; nor about your body, what you will put on. Is not life more than food and the body more than clothing? ²⁶Look at the birds of the air, for they neither sow nor reap nor gather into barns; yet your heavenly Father feeds them. Are you not of more value than they? ²⁷Which of you by worrying can add one cubit to his stature?

²⁸"So why do you worry about clothing? Consider the lilies of the field, how they grow: they neither toil nor spin; ²⁹and yet I say to you that even Solomon in all his glory was not arrayed like one of these. ³⁰Now if God so clothes the grass of the field, which today is, and tomorrow is thrown into the oven, will He not much more clothe you, O you of little faith?

³¹"Therefore do not worry, saying, 'What shall we eat?' or 'What shall we drink?' or 'What shall we wear?'"

Matt 7:1-28 ¹"Judge not, that you be not judged. ²For with what judgment you judge, you will be judged; and with the measure you use, it will be measured back to you. ³And why do you look at the speck in your brother's eye, but do not consider the plank in your own eye? ⁴Or how can you say to your brother, 'Let me remove the speck from your eye'; and look, a plank is in your own eye? ⁵Hypocrite! First remove the plank from your own eye, and then you will see clearly to remove the speck from your brother's eye.

⁶"Do not give what is holy to the dogs; nor cast your pearls before swine, lest they trample them under their feet, and turn and tear you in pieces.

⁷"Ask, and it will be given to you; seek, and you will find; knock, and it will be opened to you. ⁸For everyone who asks receives, and he who seeks finds, and to him who knocks it will be opened. ⁹Or what man is there among you who, if his son asks for bread, will give him a stone? ¹⁰Or if he asks for a fish, will he give him a serpent? ¹¹If you then, being evil, know how to give good gifts to your children, how much more will your Father who is in heaven give good things to those who ask Him! ¹²Therefore, whatever you want men to do to you, do also to them, for this is the Law and the Prophets.

¹³"Enter by the narrow gate; for wide is the gate and broad is the way that leads to destruction, and there are many who go in by it. ¹⁴Because narrow is the gate and difficult is the way which leads to life, and there are few who find it.

¹⁵"Beware of false prophets, who come to you in sheep's clothing, but inwardly they are ravenous wolves. ¹⁶You will know them by their fruits. Do men gather grapes from thornbushes or figs from thistles? ¹⁷Even so, every good tree bears good fruit, but a bad tree bears bad fruit. ¹⁸A good tree cannot bear bad fruit, nor can a bad tree bear good fruit. ¹⁹Every tree that does not bear good fruit is cut down and thrown into the fire. ²⁰Therefore by their fruits you will know them.

²¹"Not everyone who says to Me, 'Lord, Lord,' shall enter the kingdom of heaven, but he who does the will of My Father in heaven. ²²Many will say to Me in that day, 'Lord, Lord, have we not prophesied in Your name, cast out demons in Your name, and done many wonders in Your name?' ²³And then I will declare to them, 'I never knew you; depart from Me, you who practice lawlessness!'

²⁴"Therefore whoever hears these sayings of Mine, and does them, I will liken him to a wise man who built his house on the rock: ²⁵and the rain descended, the floods came, and the winds blew and beat on that house; and it did not fall, for it was founded on the rock.

²⁶"But everyone who hears these sayings of Mine, and does not do them, will be like a foolish man who built his house on the sand: ²⁷and the rain descended, the floods came, and the winds blew and beat on that house; and it fell. And great was its fall."

²⁸And so it was, when Jesus had ended these sayings, that the people were astonished at His teaching.

48 Humble Officer's Son Healed

Lk 7:1-5 ¹Now when He concluded all His sayings in the hearing of the people, He entered Capernaum. ²And a certain centurion's servant, who was dear to him, was sick and ready to die. ³So when he heard about Jesus, he sent elders of the Jews to Him, pleading with Him to come and heal his servant. ⁴And when they came to Jesus, they begged Him earnestly, saying that the one for whom He should do this was deserving, ⁵"for he loves our nation, and has built us a synagogue."

Matt 8:7 ⁷And Jesus said to him, "I will come and heal him."

Lk 7:6-9 ⁶Then Jesus went with them. And when He was already not far from the house, the centurion sent friends to Him, saying to Him, "Lord, do not trouble Yourself, for I am not worthy that You should enter under my roof. ⁷Therefore I did not even think myself worthy to come to You. But say the word, and my servant will be healed. ⁸For I also am a man placed under authority, having soldiers under me. And I say to one, 'Go,' and he goes; and to another, 'Come,' and he comes; and to my servant, 'Do this,' and he does it."

⁹When Jesus heard these things, He marveled at him, and turned around and said to the crowd

that followed Him, "I say to you, I have not found such great faith, not even in Israel!"

Matt 8:11-13 [11] "And I say to you that many will come from east and west, and sit down with Abraham, Isaac, and Jacob in the kingdom of heaven. [12] But the sons of the kingdom will be cast out into outer darkness. There will be weeping and gnashing of teeth." [13] Then Jesus said to the centurion, "Go your way; and as you have believed, so let it be done for you." And his servant was healed that same hour.

49. Life Restored to Widow's Son

Lk 7:11-17 [11] Now it happened, the day after, that He went into a city called Nain; and many of His disciples went with Him, and a large crowd. [12] And when He came near the gate of the city, behold, a dead man was being carried out, the only son of his mother; and she was a widow. And a large crowd from the city was with her. [13] When the Lord saw her, He had compassion on her and said to her, "Do not weep." [14] Then He came and touched the open coffin, and those who carried him stood still. And He said, "Young man, I say to you, arise." [15] So he who was dead sat up and began to speak. And He presented him to his mother.

[16] Then fear came upon all, and they glorified God, saying, "A great prophet has risen up among us"; and, "God has visited His people." [17] And this report about Him went throughout all Judea and all the surrounding region.

50. John Inquires Regarding Jesus' Messiahship

Lk 7:18-35 [18]Then the disciples of John reported to him concerning all these things. [19]And John, calling two of his disciples to him, sent them to Jesus, saying, "Are You the Coming One, or do we look for another?"

[20]When the men had come to Him, they said, "John the Baptist has sent us to You, saying, 'Are You the Coming One, or do we look for another?'" [21]And that very hour He cured many of infirmities, afflictions, and evil spirits; and to many blind He gave sight.

[22]Jesus answered and said to them, "Go and tell John the things you have seen and heard: that the blind see, the lame walk, the lepers are cleansed, the deaf hear, the dead are raised, the poor have the gospel preached to them. [23]And blessed is he who is not offended because of Me."

[24]When the messengers of John had departed, He began to speak to the multitudes concerning John: "What did you go out into the wilderness to see? A reed shaken by the wind? [25]But what did you go out to see? A man clothed in soft garments? Indeed those who are gorgeously appareled and live in luxury are in kings' courts. [26]But what did you go out to see? A prophet? Yes, I say to you, and more than a prophet. [27]This is he of whom it is written:

'Behold, I send My messenger before Your face,
Who will prepare Your way before You.'

²⁸For I say to you, among those born of women there is not a greater prophet than John the Baptist; but he who is least in the kingdom of God is greater than he."

²⁹And when all the people heard Him, even the tax collectors justified God, having been baptized with the baptism of John. ³⁰But the Pharisees and lawyers rejected the will of God for themselves, not having been baptized by him.

³¹And the Lord said, "To what then shall I liken the men of this generation, and what are they like? ³²They are like children sitting in the marketplace and calling to one another, saying:

'We played the flute for you,
    And you did not dance;
We mourned to you,
    And you did not weep.'

³³For John the Baptist came neither eating bread nor drinking wine, and you say, 'He has a demon.' ³⁴The Son of Man has come eating and drinking, and you say, 'Look, a glutton and a winebibber, a friend of tax collectors and sinners!' ³⁵But wisdom is justified by all her children."

51. Jesus Issues an Invitation to Everyone

Matt 11:20-30 ²⁰Then He began to rebuke the cities in which most of His mighty works had been done, because they did not repent: ²¹"Woe to you, Chorazin! Woe to you, Bethsaida! For if the mighty works which were done in you had been done in Tyre and Sidon, they would have repented long ago in sackcloth and ashes. ²²But I say to you, it will be more tolerable for Tyre and Sidon in the day of judgment than for you. ²³And you, Capernaum, who are exalted to heaven, will be brought down to Hades; for if the mighty works which were done in you had been done in Sodom, it would have remained until this day. ²⁴But I say to you that it shall be more tolerable for the land of Sodom in the day of judgment than for you."

²⁵At that time Jesus answered and said, "I thank You, Father, Lord of heaven and earth, that You have hidden these things from the wise and prudent and have revealed them to babes. ²⁶Even so, Father, for so it seemed good in Your sight. ²⁷All things have been delivered to Me by My Father, and no one knows the Son except the Father. Nor does anyone know the Father except the Son, and the one to whom the Son wills to reveal Him. ²⁸Come to Me, all you who labor and are heavy laden, and I will give you rest. ²⁹Take My yoke upon you and learn from Me, for I am gentle and lowly in

heart, and you will find rest for your souls. ³⁰For My yoke is easy and My burden is light."

52. Women Support Jesus and the Disciples

Lk 8:1-3 ¹Now it came to pass, afterward, that He went through every city and village, preaching and bringing the glad tidings of the kingdom of God. And the twelve were with Him, ²and certain women who had been healed of evil spirits and infirmities—Mary called Magdalene, out of whom had come seven demons, ³and Joanna the wife of Chuza, Herod's steward, and Susanna, and many others who provided for Him from their substance.

53. Honesty Costs John His Life

Mk 6:21-29 ²¹Then an opportune day came when Herod on his birthday gave a feast for his nobles, the high officers, and the chief men of Galilee. ²²And when Herodias' daughter herself came in and danced, and pleased Herod and those who sat with him, the king said to the girl, "Ask me whatever you want, and I will give it to you." ²³He also swore to her, "Whatever you ask me, I will give you, up to half my kingdom."

²⁴So she went out and said to her mother, "What shall I ask?"

And she said, "The head of John the Baptist!"

²⁵Immediately she came in with haste to the king and asked, saying, "I want you to give me at once the head of John the Baptist on a platter."

²⁶And the king was exceedingly sorry; yet, because of the oaths and because of those who sat with him, he did not want to refuse her. ²⁷Immediately the king sent an executioner and commanded his head to be brought. And he went and beheaded him in prison, ²⁸brought his head on a platter, and gave it to the girl; and the girl gave it to her mother. ²⁹When his disciples heard of it, they came and took away his corpse and laid it in a tomb.

54. Jesus Meets Opposition

Mk 3:20–21 ²⁰Then the multitude came together again, so that they could not so much as eat bread. ²¹But when His own people heard about this, they went out to lay hold of Him, for they said, "He is out of His mind."

Matt 12:22–50 ²²Then one was brought to Him who was demon-possessed, blind and mute; and He healed him, so that the blind and mute man both spoke and saw. ²³And all the multitudes were amazed and said, "Could this be the Son of David?"

²⁴Now when the Pharisees heard it they said, "This fellow does not cast out demons except by Beelzebub, the ruler of the demons."

²⁵But Jesus knew their thoughts, and said to them: "Every kingdom divided against itself is brought to desolation, and every city or house divided against itself will not stand. ²⁶If Satan casts out Satan, he is divided against himself. How then will his kingdom stand? ²⁷And if I cast out demons

by Beelzebub, by whom do your sons cast them out? Therefore they shall be your judges. ²⁸But if I cast out demons by the Spirit of God, surely the kingdom of God has come upon you. ²⁹Or how can one enter a strong man's house and plunder his goods, unless he first binds the strong man? And then he will plunder his house. ³⁰He who is not with Me is against Me, and he who does not gather with Me scatters abroad.

³¹"Therefore I say to you, every sin and blasphemy will be forgiven men, but the blasphemy against the Spirit will not be forgiven men. ³²Anyone who speaks a word against the Son of Man, it will be forgiven him; but whoever speaks against the Holy Spirit, it will not be forgiven him, either in this age or in the age to come.

³³"Either make the tree good and its fruit good, or else make the tree bad and its fruit bad; for a tree is known by its fruit. ³⁴Brood of vipers! How can you, being evil, speak good things? For out of the abundance of the heart the mouth speaks. ³⁵A good man out of the good treasure of his heart brings forth good things, and an evil man out of the evil treasure brings forth evil things. ³⁶But I say to you that for every idle word men may speak, they will give account of it in the day of judgment. ³⁷For by your words you will be justified, and by your words you will be condemned."

³⁸Then some of the scribes and Pharisees answered, saying, "Teacher, we want to see a sign from You."

³⁹But He answered and said to them, "An evil and adulterous generation seeks after a sign, and no sign will be given to it except the sign of the prophet Jonah. ⁴⁰For as Jonah was three days and three nights in the belly of the great fish, so will the Son of Man be three days and three nights in the heart of the earth. ⁴¹The men of Nineveh will rise up in the judgment with this generation and condemn it, because they repented at the preaching of Jonah; and indeed a greater than Jonah is here. ⁴²The queen of the South will rise up in the judgment with this generation and condemn it, for she came from the ends of the earth to hear the wisdom of Solomon; and indeed a greater than Solomon is here.

⁴³"When an unclean spirit goes out of a man, he goes through dry places, seeking rest, and finds none. ⁴⁴Then he says, 'I will return to my house from which I came.' And when he comes, he finds it empty, swept, and put in order. ⁴⁵Then he goes and takes with him seven other spirits more wicked than himself, and they enter and dwell there; and the last state of that man is worse than the first. So shall it also be with this wicked generation."

⁴⁶While He was still talking to the multitudes, behold, His mother and brothers stood outside, seeking to speak with Him. ⁴⁷Then one said to Him, "Look, Your mother and Your brothers are standing outside, seeking to speak with You."

⁴⁸But He answered and said to the one who told Him, "Who is My mother and who are My

brothers?" ⁴⁹And He stretched out His hand toward His disciples and said, "Here are My mother and My brothers! ⁵⁰For whoever does the will of My Father in heaven is My brother and sister and mother."

55. Earthly Stories with Heavenly Meaning

Mk 4:1–12 ¹And again He began to teach by the sea. And a great multitude was gathered to Him, so that He got into a boat and sat in it on the sea; and the whole multitude was on the land facing the sea. ²Then He taught them many things by parables, and said to them in His teaching:

³"Listen! Behold, a sower went out to sow. ⁴And it happened, as he sowed, that some seed fell by the wayside; and the birds of the air came and devoured it. ⁵Some fell on stony ground, where it did not have much earth; and immediately it sprang up because it had no depth of earth. ⁶But when the sun was up it was scorched, and because it had no root it withered away. ⁷And some seed fell among thorns; and the thorns grew up and choked it, and it yielded no crop. ⁸But other seed fell on good ground and yielded a crop that sprang up, increased and produced: some thirtyfold, some sixty, and some a hundred."

⁹And He said to them, "He who has ears to hear, let him hear!"

¹⁰But when He was alone, those around Him with the twelve asked Him about the parable.

¹¹And He said to them, "To you it has been given to know the mystery of the kingdom of God; but to those who are outside, all things come in parables, ¹²so that

> 'Seeing they may see and not perceive,
> And hearing they may hear and not
>   understand;
> Lest they should turn,
> And their sins be forgiven them.'"

Matt 13:14–17 ¹⁴"And in them the prophecy of Isaiah is fulfilled, which says:

> 'Hearing you will hear and shall not
>   understand,
> And seeing you will see and not perceive;
> ¹⁵ For the hearts of this people have grown
>   dull.
> Their ears are hard of hearing,
> And their eyes they have closed,
> Lest they should see with their eyes and
>   hear with their ears,
> Lest they should understand with their
>   hearts and turn,
> So that I should heal them.'

¹⁶But blessed are your eyes for they see, and your ears for they hear; ¹⁷for assuredly, I say to you that many prophets and righteous men desired to see

what you see, and did not see it, and to hear what you hear, and did not hear it."

Mk 4:13–34 [13] And He said to them, "Do you not understand this parable? How then will you understand all the parables? [14] The sower sows the word. [15] And these are the ones by the wayside where the word is sown. When they hear, Satan comes immediately and takes away the word that was sown in their hearts. [16] These likewise are the ones sown on stony ground who, when they hear the word, immediately receive it with gladness; [17] and they have no root in themselves, and so endure only for a time. Afterward, when tribulation or persecution arises for the word's sake, immediately they stumble. [18] Now these are the ones sown among thorns; they are the ones who hear the word, [19] and the cares of this world, the deceitfulness of riches, and the desires for other things entering in choke the word, and it becomes unfruitful. [20] But these are the ones sown on good ground, those who hear the word, accept it, and bear fruit: some thirtyfold, some sixty, and some a hundred."

[21] Also He said to them, "Is a lamp brought to be put under a basket or under a bed? Is it not to be set on a lampstand? [22] For there is nothing hidden which will not be revealed, nor has anything been kept secret but that it should come to light. [23] If anyone has ears to hear, let him hear."

[24] Then He said to them, "Take heed what you hear. With the same measure you use, it will be measured to you; and to you who hear, more will

be given. ²⁵For whoever has, to him more will be given; but whoever does not have, even what he has will be taken away from him."

²⁶And He said, "The kingdom of God is as if a man should scatter seed on the ground, ²⁷and should sleep by night and rise by day, and the seed should sprout and grow, he himself does not know how. ²⁸For the earth yields crops by itself: first the blade, then the head, after that the full grain in the head. ²⁹But when the grain ripens, immediately he puts in the sickle, because the harvest has come."

³⁰Then He said, "To what shall we liken the kingdom of God? Or with what parable shall we picture it? ³¹It is like a mustard seed which, when it is sown on the ground, is smaller than all the seeds on earth; ³²but when it is sown, it grows up and becomes greater than all herbs, and shoots out large branches, so that the birds of the air may nest under its shade."

³³And with many such parables He spoke the word to them as they were able to hear it. ³⁴But without a parable He did not speak to them. And when they were alone, He explained all things to His disciples.

Matt 13:35–53 ³⁵That it might be fulfilled which was spoken by the prophet, saying:

"I will open My mouth in parables;
I will utter things kept secret from the
foundation of the world."

³⁶Then Jesus sent the multitude away and went into the house. And His disciples came to Him, saying, "Explain to us the parable of the tares of the field."

³⁷He answered and said to them: "He who sows the good seed is the Son of Man. ³⁸The field is the world, the good seeds are the sons of the kingdom, but the tares are the sons of the wicked one. ³⁹The enemy who sowed them is the devil, the harvest is the end of the age, and the reapers are the angels. ⁴⁰Therefore as the tares are gathered and burned in the fire, so it will be at the end of this age. ⁴¹The Son of Man will send out His angels, and they will gather out of His kingdom all things that offend, and those who practice lawlessness, ⁴²and will cast them into the furnace of fire. There will be wailing and gnashing of teeth. ⁴³Then the righteous will shine forth as the sun in the kingdom of their Father. He who has ears to hear, let him hear!

⁴⁴"Again, the kingdom of heaven is like treasure hidden in a field, which a man found and hid; and for joy over it he goes and sells all that he has and buys that field.

⁴⁵"Again, the kingdom of heaven is like a merchant seeking beautiful pearls, ⁴⁶who, when he had found one pearl of great price, went and sold all that he had and bought it.

⁴⁷"Again, the kingdom of heaven is like a dragnet that was cast into the sea and gathered some of every kind, ⁴⁸which, when it was full, they drew to

shore; and they sat down and gathered the good into vessels, but threw the bad away. ⁴⁹So it will be at the end of the age. The angels will come forth, separate the wicked from among the just, ⁵⁰and cast them into the furnace of fire. There will be wailing and gnashing of teeth."

⁵¹Jesus said to them, "Have you understood all these things?"

They said to Him, "Yes, Lord."

⁵²Then He said to them, "Therefore every scribe instructed concerning the kingdom of heaven is like a householder who brings out of his treasure things new and old."

⁵³Now it came to pass, when Jesus had finished these parables, that He departed from there.

56. Jesus Rebukes the Elements

Mk 4:35–41 ³⁵On the same day, when evening had come, He said to them, "Let us cross over to the other side." ³⁶Now when they had left the multitude, they took Him along in the boat as He was. And other little boats were also with Him. ³⁷And a great windstorm arose, and the waves beat into the boat, so that it was already filling. ³⁸But He was in the stern, asleep on a pillow. And they awoke Him and said to Him, "Teacher, do You not care that we are perishing?"

³⁹Then He arose and rebuked the wind, and said to the sea, "Peace, be still!" And the wind ceased and there was a great calm. ⁴⁰But He said to them, "Why are you so fearful? How is it that you

have no faith?" ⁴¹And they feared exceedingly, and said to one another, "Who can this be, that even the wind and the sea obey Him!"

57. Devils Listen to Jesus

Mk 5:1-20 ¹Then they came to the other side of the sea, to the country of the Gadarenes. ²And when He had come out of the boat, immediately there met Him out of the tombs a man with an unclean spirit, ³who had his dwelling among the tombs; and no one could bind him, not even with chains, ⁴because he had often been bound with shackles and chains. And the chains had been pulled apart by him, and the shackles broken in pieces; neither could anyone tame him. ⁵And always, night and day, he was in the mountains and in the tombs, crying out and cutting himself with stones.

⁶When he saw Jesus from afar, he ran and worshiped Him. ⁷And he cried out with a loud voice and said, "What have I to do with You, Jesus, Son of the Most High God? I implore You by God that You do not torment me."

⁸For He said to him, "Come out of the man, unclean spirit!" ⁹Then He asked him, "What is your name?"

And he answered, saying, "My name is Legion; for we are many." ¹⁰Also he begged Him earnestly that He would not send them out of the country.

¹¹Now a large herd of swine was feeding there near the mountains. ¹²So all the demons begged

Him, saying, "Send us to the swine, that we may enter them." [13]And at once Jesus gave them permission. Then the unclean spirits went out and entered the swine (there were about two thousand); and the herd ran violently down the steep place into the sea, and drowned in the sea.

[14]So those who fed the swine fled, and they told it in the city and in the country. And they went out to see what it was that had happened. [15]Then they came to Jesus, and saw the one who had been demon-possessed and had the legion, sitting and clothed and in his right mind. And they were afraid. [16]And those who saw it told them how it happened to him who had been demon-possessed, and about the swine. [17]Then they began to plead with Him to depart from their region.

[18]And when He got into the boat, he who had been demon-possessed begged Him that he might be with Him. [19]However, Jesus did not permit him, but said to him, "Go home to your friends, and tell them what great things the Lord has done for you, and how He has had compassion on you." [20]And he departed and began to proclaim in Decapolis all that Jesus had done for him; and all marveled.

58. "The Touch of the Master's Hand"

Mk 5:21–32 [21]Now when Jesus had crossed over again by boat to the other side, a great multitude gathered to Him; and He was by the sea. [22]And behold, one of the rulers of the synagogue came,

Jairus by name. And when he saw Him, he fell at His feet ²³and begged Him earnestly, saying, "My little daughter lies at the point of death. Come and lay Your hands on her, that she may be healed, and she will live." ²⁴So Jesus went with him, and a great multitude followed Him and thronged Him.

²⁵Now a certain woman had a flow of blood for twelve years, ²⁶and had suffered many things from many physicians. She had spent all that she had and was no better, but rather grew worse. ²⁷When she heard about Jesus, she came behind Him in the crowd and touched His garment. ²⁸For she said, "If only I may touch His clothes, I shall be made well."

²⁹Immediately the fountain of her blood was dried up, and she felt in her body that she was healed of the affliction. ³⁰And Jesus, immediately knowing in Himself that power had gone out of Him, turned around in the crowd and said, "Who touched My clothes?"

³¹But His disciples said to Him, "You see the multitude thronging You, and You say, 'Who touched Me?'"

³²And He looked around to see her who had done this thing.

Lk 8:46–53 ⁴⁶But Jesus said, "Somebody touched Me, for I perceived power going out from Me." ⁴⁷Now when the woman saw that she was not hidden, she came trembling; and falling down before Him, she declared to Him in the presence of all the people the reason she had touched Him and how she was healed immediately.

⁴⁸And He said to her, "Daughter, be of good cheer; your faith has made you well. Go in peace."

⁴⁹While He was still speaking, someone came from the ruler of the synagogue's house, saying to him, "Your daughter is dead. Do not trouble the Teacher."

⁵⁰But when Jesus heard it, He answered him, saying, "Do not be afraid; only believe, and she will be made well." ⁵¹When He came into the house, He permitted no one to go in except Peter, James, and John, and the father and mother of the girl. ⁵²Now all wept and mourned for her; but He said, "Do not weep; she is not dead, but sleeping." ⁵³And they ridiculed Him, knowing that she was dead.

Mk 5:40-43 ⁴⁰And they ridiculed Him. But when He had put them all outside, He took the father and the mother of the child, and those who were with Him, and entered where the child was lying. ⁴¹Then He took the child by the hand, and said to her, "Talitha, cumi," which is translated, "Little girl, I say to you, arise." ⁴²Immediately the girl arose and walked, for she was twelve years of age. And they were overcome with great amazement. ⁴³But He commanded them strictly that no one should know it, and said that something should be given her to eat.

Matt 9:26 ²⁶And the report of this went out into all that land.

59. Jesus Makes Eyes See, Lips Speak

Matt 9:27–34 ²⁷When Jesus departed from there, two blind men followed Him, crying out and saying, "Son of David, have mercy on us!"

²⁸And when He had come into the house, the blind men came to Him. And Jesus said to them, "Do you believe that I am able to do this?"

They said to Him, "Yes, Lord."

²⁹Then He touched their eyes, saying, "According to your faith let it be to you." ³⁰And their eyes were opened. And Jesus sternly warned them, saying, "See that no one knows it." ³¹But when they had departed, they spread the news about Him in all that country.

³²As they went out, behold, they brought to Him a man, mute and demon-possessed. ³³And when the demon was cast out, the mute spoke. And the multitudes marveled, saying, "It was never seen like this in Israel!"

³⁴But the Pharisees said, "He casts out demons by the ruler of the demons."

60. Nazareth Rejects Local Son

Mk 6:1–6 ¹Then He went out from there and came to His own country, and His disciples followed Him. ²And when the Sabbath had come, He began to teach in the synagogue. And many hearing Him were astonished, saying, "Where did this Man get these things? And what wisdom is this which is given to Him, that such mighty works are performed by His hands! ³Is this not the carpenter, the Son of Mary, and brother of James, Joses, Judas, and Simon? And are not His sisters here with us?" So they were offended at Him.

⁴But Jesus said to them, "A prophet is not without honor except in his own country, among his own relatives, and in his own house." ⁵Now He could do no mighty work there, except that He laid His hands on a few sick people and healed them. ⁶And He marveled because of their unbelief. Then He went about the villages in a circuit, teaching.

Matt 9:35–38 ³⁵Then Jesus went about all the cities and villages, teaching in their synagogues, preaching the gospel of the kingdom, and healing every sickness and every disease among the people. ³⁶But when He saw the multitudes, He was moved with compassion for them, because they were weary and scattered, like sheep having no shepherd. ³⁷Then He said to His disciples, "The harvest truly is plentiful, but the laborers are few. ³⁸Therefore pray the Lord of the harvest to send out laborers into His harvest."

61. New Mission Territory for the Twelve

Matt 10:1–42 ¹And when He had called His twelve disciples to Him, He gave them power over unclean spirits, to cast them out, and to heal all kinds of sickness and all kinds of disease. ²Now the names of the twelve apostles are these: first, Simon, who is called Peter, and Andrew his brother;

James the son of Zebedee, and John his brother; [3]Philip and Bartholomew; Thomas and Matthew the tax collector; James the son of Alphaeus, and Lebbaeus, whose surname was Thaddaeus; [4]Simon the Cananite, and Judas Iscariot, who also betrayed Him.

[5]These twelve Jesus sent out and commanded them, saying: "Do not go into the way of the Gentiles, and do not enter a city of the Samaritans. [6]But go rather to the lost sheep of the house of Israel. [7]And as you go, preach, saying, 'The kingdom of heaven is at hand.' [8]Heal the sick, cleanse the lepers, raise the dead, cast out demons. Freely you have received, freely give. [9]Provide neither gold nor silver nor copper in your money belts, [10]nor bag for your journey, nor two tunics, nor sandals, nor staffs; for a worker is worthy of his food.

[11]"Now whatever city or town you enter, inquire who in it is worthy, and stay there till you go out. [12]And when you go into a household, greet it. [13]If the household is worthy, let your peace come upon it. But if it is not worthy, let your peace return to you. [14]And whoever will not receive you nor hear your words, when you depart from that house or city, shake off the dust from your feet. [15]Assuredly, I say to you, it will be more tolerable for the land of Sodom and Gomorrah in the day of judgment than for that city!

[16]"Behold, I send you out as sheep in the midst of wolves. Therefore be wise as serpents and harm-

less as doves. ¹⁷But beware of men, for they will deliver you up to councils and scourge you in their synagogues. ¹⁸You will be brought before governors and kings for My sake, as a testimony to them and to the Gentiles. ¹⁹But when they deliver you up, do not worry about how or what you should speak. For it will be given to you in that hour what you should speak; ²⁰for it is not you who speak, but the Spirit of your Father who speaks in you.

²¹"Now brother will deliver up brother to death, and a father his child; and children will rise up against parents and cause them to be put to death. ²²And you will be hated by all for My name's sake. But he who endures to the end will be saved. ²³When they persecute you in this city, flee to another. For assuredly, I say to you, you will not have gone through the cities of Israel before the Son of Man comes.

²⁴"A disciple is not above his teacher, nor a servant above his master. ²⁵It is enough for a disciple that he be like his teacher, and a servant like his master. If they have called the master of the house Beelzebub, how much more will they call those of his household! ²⁶Therefore do not fear them. For there is nothing covered that will not be revealed, and hidden that will not be known.

²⁷"Whatever I tell you in the dark, speak in the light; and what you hear in the ear, preach on the housetops. ²⁸And do not fear those who kill the body but cannot kill the soul. But rather fear Him who is able to destroy both soul and body in hell.

²⁹Are not two sparrows sold for a copper coin? And not one of them falls to the ground apart from your Father's will. ³⁰But the very hairs of your head are all numbered. ³¹Do not fear therefore; you are of more value than many sparrows.

³²"Therefore whoever confesses Me before men, him I will also confess before My Father who is in heaven. ³³But whoever denies Me before men, him I will also deny before My Father who is in heaven.

³⁴"Do not think that I came to bring peace on earth. I did not come to bring peace but a sword. ³⁵For I have come to 'set a man against his father, a daughter against her mother, and a daughter-in-law against her mother-in-law'; ³⁶and 'a man's enemies will be those of his own household.' ³⁷He who loves father or mother more than Me is not worthy of Me. And he who loves son or daughter more than Me is not worthy of Me. ³⁸And he who does not take his cross and follow after Me is not worthy of Me. ³⁹He who finds his life will lose it, and he who loses his life for My sake will find it.

⁴⁰"He who receives you receives Me, and he who receives Me receives Him who sent Me. ⁴¹He who receives a prophet in the name of a prophet shall receive a prophet's reward. And he who receives a righteous man in the name of a righteous man shall receive a righteous man's reward. ⁴²And whoever gives one of these little ones only a cup of cold water in the name of a disciple, assuredly, I say to you, he shall by no means lose his reward."

Mk 6:12-13 ¹²So they went out and preached that people should repent. ¹³And they cast out many demons, and anointed with oil many who were sick, and healed them.

62. A King Fears the Christ

Mk 6:14-15 ¹⁴Now King Herod heard of Him, for His name had become well known. And he said, "John the Baptist is risen from the dead, and therefore these powers are at work in him."

¹⁵Others said, "It is Elijah."

And others said, "It is the Prophet, or like one of the prophets."

Lk 9:9 ⁹Herod said, "John I have beheaded, but who is this of whom I hear such things?" So he sought to see Him.

63. The Twelve Complete Their Mission

Mk 6:30 ³⁰Then the apostles gathered to Jesus and told Him all things, both what they had done and what they had taught.

JESUS VENTURES
FROM GALILEE

64. A Boat Provides Rest

Mk 6:31-33 ³¹And He said to them, "Come aside by yourselves to a deserted place and rest a while." For there were many coming and going, and they did not even have time to eat. ³²So they departed to a deserted place in the boat by themselves.

³³But the multitudes saw them departing, and many knew Him and ran there on foot from all the cities. They arrived before them and came together to Him.

65. Five Thousand Fed by a Miracle

Jn 6:3-13 ³And Jesus went up on the mountain, and there He sat with His disciples.

⁴Now the Passover, a feast of the Jews, was near. ⁵Then Jesus lifted up His eyes, and seeing a great multitude coming toward Him, He said to

Philip, "Where shall we buy bread, that these may eat?" ⁶But this He said to test him, for He Himself knew what He would do.

⁷Philip answered Him, "Two hundred denarii worth of bread is not sufficient for them, that every one of them may have a little."

⁸One of His disciples, Andrew, Simon Peter's brother, said to Him, ⁹"There is a lad here who has five barley loaves and two small fish, but what are they among so many?"

¹⁰Then Jesus said, "Make the people sit down." Now there was much grass in the place. So the men sat down, in number about five thousand. ¹¹And Jesus took the loaves, and when He had given thanks He distributed them to the disciples, and the disciples to those sitting down; and likewise of the fish, as much as they wanted. ¹²So when they were filled, He said to His disciples, "Gather up the fragments that remain, so that nothing is lost." ¹³Therefore they gathered them up, and filled twelve baskets with the fragments of the five barley loaves which were left over by those who had eaten.

66. Jesus Treads on Watery Path

Matt 14:22-33 ²²Immediately Jesus made His disciples get into the boat and go before Him to the other side, while He sent the multitudes away. ²³And when He had sent the multitudes away, He went up on the mountain by Himself to pray. Now when evening came, He was alone there. ²⁴But the boat was now in the middle of the sea, tossed by the waves, for the wind was contrary.

²⁵Now in the fourth watch of the night Jesus went to them, walking on the sea. ²⁶And when the disciples saw Him walking on the sea, they were troubled, saying, "It is a ghost!" And they cried out for fear.

²⁷But immediately Jesus spoke to them, saying, "Be of good cheer! It is I; do not be afraid."

²⁸And Peter answered Him and said, "Lord, if it is You, command me to come to You on the water."

²⁹So He said, "Come." And when Peter had come down out of the boat, he walked on the water to go to Jesus. ³⁰But when he saw that the wind was boisterous, he was afraid; and beginning to sink he cried out, saying, "Lord, save me!"

³¹And immediately Jesus stretched out His hand and caught him, and said to him, "O you of little faith, why did you doubt?" ³²And when they got into the boat, the wind ceased.

³³Then those who were in the boat came and worshiped Him, saying, "Truly You are the Son of God."

Mk 6:51-52 ⁵¹Then He went up into the boat to them, and the wind ceased. And they were greatly amazed in themselves beyond measure, and marveled. ⁵²For they had not understood about the loaves, because their heart was hardened.

67. Jesus Continues Healing in Gennesaret

Mk 6:53-56 ⁵³When they had crossed over, they came to the land of Gennesaret and anchored there. ⁵⁴And when they came out of the boat, immediately the people recognized Him, ⁵⁵ran through that whole surrounding region, and began to carry about on beds those who were sick to wherever they heard He was. ⁵⁶Wherever He entered, into villages, cities, or the country, they laid the sick in the marketplaces, and begged Him that they might just touch the hem of His garment. And as many as touched Him were made well

68. An Answer to Hunger and Thirst

Jn 6:22-71 ²²On the following day, when the people who were standing on the other side of the sea saw that there was no other boat there, except that one which His disciples had entered, and that Jesus had not entered the boat with His disciples, but His disciples had gone away alone— ²³however, other boats came from Tiberias, near the place where they ate bread after the Lord had given thanks— ²⁴when the people therefore saw that Jesus was not there, nor His disciples, they also got into boats and came to Capernaum, seeking Jesus. ²⁵And when they found Him on the other side of the sea, they said to Him, "Rabbi, when did You come here?"

²⁶Jesus answered them and said, "Most

assuredly, I say to you, you seek Me, not because you saw the signs, but because you ate of the loaves and were filled. ²⁷Do not labor for the food which perishes, but for the food which endures to everlasting life, which the Son of Man will give you, because God the Father has set His seal on Him."

²⁸Then they said to Him, "What shall we do, that we may work the works of God?"

²⁹Jesus answered and said to them, "This is the work of God, that you believe in Him whom He sent."

³⁰Therefore they said to Him, "What sign will You perform then, that we may see it and believe You? What work will You do? ³¹Our fathers ate the manna in the desert; as it is written, 'He gave them bread from heaven to eat.'"

³²Then Jesus said to them, "Most assuredly, I say to you, Moses did not give you the bread from heaven, but My Father gives you the true bread from heaven. ³³For the bread of God is He who comes down from heaven and gives life to the world."

³⁴Then they said to Him, "Lord, give us this bread always."

³⁵And Jesus said to them, "I am the bread of life. He who comes to Me shall never hunger, and he who believes in Me shall never thirst. ³⁶But I said to you that you have seen Me and yet do not believe. ³⁷All that the Father gives Me will come to Me, and the one who comes to Me I will by no

means cast out. ³⁸For I have come down from heaven, not to do My own will, but the will of Him who sent Me. ³⁹This is the will of the Father who sent Me, that of all He has given Me I should lose nothing, but should raise it up at the last day. ⁴⁰And this is the will of Him who sent Me, that everyone who sees the Son and believes in Him may have everlasting life; and I will raise him up at the last day."

⁴¹The Jews then complained about Him, because He said, "I am the bread which came down from heaven." ⁴²And they said, "Is not this Jesus, the son of Joseph, whose father and mother we know? How is it then that He says, 'I have come down from heaven'?"

⁴³Jesus therefore answered and said to them, "Do not murmur among yourselves. ⁴⁴No one can come to Me unless the Father who sent Me draws him; and I will raise him up at the last day. ⁴⁵It is written in the prophets, 'And they shall all be taught by God.' Therefore everyone who has heard and learned from the Father comes to Me. ⁴⁶Not that anyone has seen the Father, except He who is from God; He has seen the Father. ⁴⁷Most assuredly, I say to you, he who believes in Me has everlasting life. ⁴⁸I am the bread of life. ⁴⁹Your fathers ate the manna in the wilderness, and are dead. ⁵⁰This is the bread which comes down from heaven, that one may eat of it and not die. ⁵¹I am the living bread which came down from heaven. If anyone eats of this bread, he will live forever; and

the bread that I shall give is My flesh, which I shall give for the life of the world."

⁵²The Jews therefore quarreled among themselves, saying, "How can this Man give us His flesh to eat?"

⁵³Then Jesus said to them, "Most assuredly, I say to you, unless you eat the flesh of the Son of Man and drink His blood, you have no life in you. ⁵⁴Whoever eats My flesh and drinks My blood has eternal life, and I will raise him up at the last day. ⁵⁵For My flesh is food indeed, and My blood is drink indeed. ⁵⁶He who eats My flesh and drinks My blood abides in Me, and I in him. ⁵⁷As the living Father sent Me, and I live because of the Father, so he who feeds on Me will live because of Me. ⁵⁸This is the bread which came down from heaven—not as your fathers ate the manna, and are dead. He who eats this bread will live forever."

⁵⁹These things He said in the synagogue as He taught in Capernaum.

⁶⁰Therefore many of His disciples, when they heard this, said, "This is a hard saying; who can understand it?"

⁶¹When Jesus knew in Himself that His disciples complained about this, He said to them, "Does this offend you? ⁶²What then if you should see the Son of Man ascend where He was before? ⁶³It is the Spirit who gives life; the flesh profits nothing. The words that I speak to you are spirit, and they are life. ⁶⁴But there are some of you who do not believe." For Jesus knew from the beginning who

they were who did not believe, and who would betray Him. ⁶⁵And He said, "Therefore I have said to you that no one can come to Me unless it has been granted to him by My Father."

⁶⁶From that time many of His disciples went back and walked with Him no more. ⁶⁷Then Jesus said to the twelve, "Do you also want to go away?"

⁶⁸But Simon Peter answered Him, "Lord, to whom shall we go? You have the words of eternal life. ⁶⁹Also we have come to believe and know that You are the Christ, the Son of the living God."

⁷⁰Jesus answered them, "Did I not choose you, the twelve, and one of you is a devil?" ⁷¹He spoke of Judas Iscariot, the son of Simon, for it was he who would betray Him, being one of the twelve.

69. What True Worship Is

Mk 7:1-23 ¹Then the Pharisees and some of the scribes came together to Him, having come from Jerusalem. ²Now when they saw some of His disciples eat bread with defiled, that is, with unwashed hands, they found fault. ³For the Pharisees and all the Jews do not eat unless they wash their hands in a special way, holding the tradition of the elders. ⁴When they come from the marketplace, they do not eat unless they wash. And there are many other things which they have received and hold, like the washing of cups, pitchers, copper vessels, and couches.

⁵Then the Pharisees and scribes asked Him,

"Why do Your disciples not walk according to the tradition of the elders, but eat bread with unwashed hands?"

⁶He answered and said to them, "Well did Isaiah prophesy of you hypocrites, as it is written:

'This people honors Me with their lips,
But their heart is far from Me.
⁷ And in vain they worship Me,
Teaching as doctrines the commandments
of men.'

⁸For laying aside the commandment of God, you hold the tradition of men—the washing of pitchers and cups, and many other such things you do."

⁹He said to them, "All too well you reject the commandment of God, that you may keep your tradition. ¹⁰For Moses said, 'Honor your father and your mother'; and, 'He who curses father or mother, let him be put to death.' ¹¹But you say, 'If a man says to his father or mother, "Whatever profit you might have received from me is Corban"—' (that is, a gift to God), ¹²then you no longer let him do anything for his father or his mother, ¹³making the word of God of no effect through your tradition which you have handed down. And many such things you do."

¹⁴When He had called all the multitude to Himself, He said to them, "Hear Me, everyone, and understand: ¹⁵There is nothing that enters a man from outside which can defile him; but the things

which come out of him, those are the things that defile a man. [16]If anyone has ears to hear, let him hear!"

[17]When He had entered a house away from the crowd, His disciples asked Him concerning the parable. [18]So He said to them, "Are you thus without understanding also? Do you not perceive that whatever enters a man from outside cannot defile him, [19]because it does not enter his heart but his stomach, and is eliminated, thus purifying all foods?" [20]And He said, "What comes out of a man, that defiles a man. [21]For from within, out of the heart of men, proceed evil thoughts, adulteries, fornications, murders, [22]thefts, covetousness, wickedness, deceit, lewdness, an evil eye, blasphemy, pride, foolishness. [23]All these evil things come from within and defile a man."

JESUS BROADENS
HEALING MINISTRY

70. *Greek Woman Exerts Her Faith*

Mk 7:24-30 ²⁴From there He arose and went to the region of Tyre and Sidon. And He entered a house and wanted no one to know it, but He could not be hidden. ²⁵For a woman whose young daughter had an unclean spirit heard about Him, and she came and fell at His feet. ²⁶The woman was a Greek, a Syro-Phoenician by birth, and she kept asking Him to cast the demon out of her daughter. ²⁷But Jesus said to her, "Let the children be filled first, for it is not good to take the children's bread and throw it to the little dogs."

²⁸And she answered and said to Him, "Yes, Lord, yet even the little dogs under the table eat from the children's crumbs."

²⁹Then He said to her, "For this saying go your way; the demon has gone out of your daughter."

³⁰And when she had come to her house, she

found the demon gone out, and her daughter lying on the bed.

71. No End to Jesus' Healings

Mk 7:31-37 ³¹Again, departing from the region of Tyre and Sidon, He came through the midst of the region of Decapolis to the Sea of Galilee. ³²Then they brought to Him one who was deaf and had an impediment in his speech, and they begged Him to put His hand on him. ³³And He took him aside from the multitude, and put His fingers in his ears, and He spat and touched his tongue. ³⁴Then, looking up to heaven, He sighed, and said to him, "Ephphatha," that is, "Be opened."

³⁵Immediately his ears were opened, and the impediment of his tongue was loosed, and he spoke plainly. ³⁶Then He commanded them that they should tell no one; but the more He commanded them, the more widely they proclaimed it. ³⁷And they were astonished beyond measure, saying, "He has done all things well. He makes both the deaf to hear and the mute to speak."

72. Four Thousand Dine with the Master

Mk 8:1-11 ¹In those days, the multitude being very great and having nothing to eat, Jesus called His disciples to Him and said to them, ²"I have compassion on the multitude, because they have now continued with Me three days and have nothing to eat. ³And if I send them away hungry to their own houses, they will faint on the way; for some of them have come from afar."

⁴Then His disciples answered Him, "How can one satisfy these people with bread here in the wilderness?"

⁵He asked them, "How many loaves do you have?"

And they said, "Seven."

⁶So He commanded the multitude to sit down on the ground. And He took the seven loaves and gave thanks, broke them and gave them to His disciples to set before them; and they set them before the multitude. ⁷They also had a few small fish; and having blessed them, He said to set them also before them. ⁸So they ate and were filled, and they took up seven large baskets of leftover fragments. ⁹Now those who had eaten were about four thousand. And He sent them away, ¹⁰immediately got into the boat with His disciples, and came to the region of Dalmanutha.

¹¹Then the Pharisees came out and began to dispute with Him, seeking from Him a sign from heaven, testing Him.

73. Jesus Teaches about Sign Interpretation

Matt 16:2-4 ²He answered and said to them, "When it is evening you say, 'It will be fair weather, for the sky is red'; ³and in the morning, 'It will be foul weather today, for the sky is red and threatening.' Hypocrites! You know how to discern the face of the sky, but you cannot discern the signs of the times. ⁴A wicked and adulterous generation seeks after a sign, and no sign shall be given to it except the sign of the prophet Jonah." And He left them and departed.

JESUS THE TEACHER IN GALILEE

74. Bread Becomes Object of Teaching

Mk 8:13-20 ¹³And He left them, and getting into the boat again, departed to the other side. ¹⁴Now the disciples had forgotten to take bread, and they did not have more than one loaf with them in the boat. ¹⁵Then He charged them, saying, "Take heed, beware of the leaven of the Pharisees and the leaven of Herod."

¹⁶And they reasoned among themselves, saying, "It is because we have no bread."

¹⁷But Jesus, being aware of it, said to them, "Why do you reason because you have no bread? Do you not yet perceive nor understand? Is your heart still hardened? ¹⁸Having eyes, do you not see? And having ears, do you not hear? And do you not remember? ¹⁹When I broke the five loaves for the five thousand, how many baskets full of fragments did you take up?"

They said to Him, "Twelve."

²⁰"Also, when I broke the seven for the four thousand, how many large baskets full of fragments did you take up?"

And they said, "Seven."

Matt 16:11–12 ¹¹"How is it you do not understand that I did not speak to you concerning bread?—but to beware of the leaven of the Pharisees and Sadducees." ¹²Then they understood that He did not tell them to beware of the leaven of bread, but of the doctrine of the Pharisees and Sadducees.

75. An Unusual Healing

Mk 8:22–26 ²²Then He came to Bethsaida; and they brought a blind man to Him, and begged Him to touch him. ²³So He took the blind man by the hand and led him out of the town. And when He had spit on his eyes and put His hands on him, He asked him if he saw anything.

²⁴And he looked up and said, "I see men like trees, walking."

²⁵Then He put His hands on his eyes again and made him look up. And he was restored and saw everyone clearly. ²⁶Then He sent him away to his house, saying, "Neither go into the town, nor tell anyone in the town."

76. Disciples Receive Testing from Jesus

Matt 16:13–20 ¹³When Jesus came into the region of Caesarea Philippi, He asked His disciples, saying, "Who do men say that I, the Son of Man, am?"

¹⁴So they said, "Some say John the Baptist, some Elijah, and others Jeremiah or one of the prophets."

¹⁵He said to them, "But who do you say that I am?"

¹⁶Simon Peter answered and said, "You are the Christ, the Son of the living God."

¹⁷Jesus answered and said to him, "Blessed are you, Simon Bar-Jonah, for flesh and blood has not revealed this to you, but My Father who is in heaven. ¹⁸And I also say to you that you are Peter, and on this rock I will build My church, and the gates of Hades shall not prevail against it. ¹⁹And I will give you the keys of the kingdom of heaven, and whatever you bind on earth will be bound in heaven, and whatever you loose on earth will be loosed in heaven."

²⁰Then He commanded His disciples that they should tell no one that He was Jesus the Christ.

77. Jesus Points to Future Events

Mk 8:31-38 ³¹And He began to teach them that the Son of Man must suffer many things, and be rejected by the elders and chief priests and scribes, and be killed, and after three days rise again. ³²He spoke this word openly. Then Peter took Him aside and began to rebuke Him. ³³But when He had turned around and looked at His disciples, He rebuked Peter, saying, "Get behind Me, Satan! For you are not mindful of the things of God, but the things of men."

³⁴When He had called the people to Himself,

with His disciples also, He said to them, "Whoever desires to come after Me, let him deny himself, and take up his cross, and follow Me. [35]For whoever desires to save his life will lose it, but whoever loses his life for My sake and the gospel's will save it. [36]For what will it profit a man if he gains the whole world, and loses his own soul? [37]Or what will a man give in exchange for his soul? [38]For whoever is ashamed of Me and My words in this adulterous and sinful generation, of him the Son of Man also will be ashamed when He comes in the glory of His Father with the holy angels."

78. God's Glory on the Mountian

Lk 9:27-36 [27]"But I tell you truly, there are some standing here who shall not taste death till they see the kingdom of God."

[28]Now it came to pass, about eight days after these sayings, that He took Peter, John, and James and went up on the mountain to pray. [29]As He prayed, the appearance of His face was altered, and His robe became white and glistening. [30]And behold, two men talked with Him, who were Moses and Elijah, [31]who appeared in glory and spoke of His decease which He was about to accomplish at Jerusalem. [32]But Peter and those with him were heavy with sleep; and when they were fully awake, they saw His glory and the two men who stood with Him. [33]Then it happened, as they were parting from Him, that Peter said to Jesus, "Master, it is good for us to be here; and let us make three

tabernacles: one for You, one for Moses, and one for Elijah"—not knowing what he said.

³⁴While he was saying this, a cloud came and overshadowed them; and they were fearful as they entered the cloud. ³⁵And a voice came out of the cloud, saying, "This is My beloved Son. Hear Him!" ³⁶When the voice had ceased, Jesus was found alone. But they kept quiet, and told no one in those days any of the things they had seen.

79. Jesus Recalls Elijah

Mk 9:9-12 ⁹Now as they came down from the mountain, He commanded them that they should tell no one the things they had seen, till the Son of Man had risen from the dead. ¹⁰So they kept this word to themselves, questioning what the rising from the dead meant.

¹¹And they asked Him, saying, "Why do the scribes say that Elijah must come first?"

¹²Then He answered and told them, "Indeed, Elijah is coming first and restores all things. And how is it written concerning the Son of Man, that He must suffer many things and be treated with contempt?"

Matt 17:12-13 ¹²"But I say to you that Elijah has come already, and they did not know him but did to him whatever they wished. Likewise the Son of Man is also about to suffer at their hands." ¹³Then the disciples understood that He spoke to them of John the Baptist.

Lk 9:36 ³⁶When the voice had ceased, Jesus was

found alone. But they kept quiet, and told no one in those days any of the things they had seen.

80. Demon Possession Conquered by Jesus

Mk 9:14-28 [14]And when He came to the disciples, He saw a great multitude around them, and scribes disputing with them. [15]Immediately, when they saw Him, all the people were greatly amazed, and running to Him, greeted Him. [16]And He asked the scribes, "What are you discussing with them?"

[17]Then one of the crowd answered and said, "Teacher, I brought You my son, who has a mute spirit. [18]And wherever it seizes him, it throws him down; he foams at the mouth, gnashes his teeth, and becomes rigid. So I spoke to Your disciples, that they should cast it out, but they could not."

[19]He answered him and said, "O faithless generation, how long shall I be with you? How long shall I bear with you? Bring him to Me." [20]Then they brought him to Him. And when he saw Him, immediately the spirit convulsed him, and he fell on the ground and wallowed, foaming at the mouth.

[21]So He asked his father, "How long has this been happening to him?"

And he said, "From childhood. [22]And often he has thrown him both into the fire and into the water to destroy him. But if You can do anything, have compassion on us and help us."

[23]Jesus said to him, "If you can believe, all things are possible to him who believes."

²⁴Immediately the father of the child cried out and said with tears, "Lord, I believe; help my unbelief!"

²⁵When Jesus saw that the people came running together, He rebuked the unclean spirit, saying to it, "Deaf and dumb spirit, I command you, come out of him and enter him no more!" ²⁶Then the spirit cried out, convulsed him greatly, and came out of him. And he became as one dead, so that many said, "He is dead." ²⁷But Jesus took him by the hand and lifted him up, and he arose.

²⁸And when He had come into the house, His disciples asked Him privately, "Why could we not cast it out?"

Matt 17:20 ²⁰So Jesus said to them, "Because of your unbelief; for assuredly, I say to you, if you have faith as a mustard seed, you will say to this mountain, 'Move from here to there,' and it will move; and nothing will be impossible for you."

Mk 9:29 ²⁹So He said to them, "This kind can come out by nothing but prayer and fasting."

81. Death Is Predicted

Mk 9:30–32 ³⁰Then they departed from there and passed through Galilee, and He did not want anyone to know it. ³¹For He taught His disciples and said to them, "The Son of Man is being betrayed into the hands of men, and they will kill Him. And after He is killed, He will rise the third day." ³²But they did not understand this saying, and were afraid to ask Him.

82. Fish's Mouth Holds Tax Money

Matt 17:24-27 ²⁴When they had come to Capernaum, those who received the temple tax came to Peter and said, "Does your Teacher not pay the temple tax?"

²⁵He said, "Yes."

And when he had come into the house, Jesus anticipated him, saying, "What do you think, Simon? From whom do the kings of the earth take customs or taxes, from their sons or from strangers?"

²⁶Peter said to Him, "From strangers."

Jesus said to him, "Then the sons are free. ²⁷Nevertheless, lest we offend them, go to the sea, cast in a hook, and take the fish that comes up first. And when you have opened its mouth, you will find a piece of money; take that and give it to them for Me and you."

83. Brothers Don't Always Know Best

Jn 7:1-9 ¹After these things Jesus walked in Galilee; for He did not want to walk in Judea, because the Jews sought to kill Him. ²Now the Jews' Feast of Tabernacles was at hand. ³His brothers therefore said to Him, "Depart from here and go into Judea, that Your disciples also may see the works that You are doing. ⁴For no one does anything in secret while he himself seeks to be known openly. If You do these things, show Yourself to the world." ⁵For even His brothers did not believe in Him.

⁶Then Jesus said to them, "My time has not yet come, but your time is always ready. ⁷The world cannot hate you, but it hates Me because I testify of it that its works are evil. ⁸You go up to this feast. I am not yet going up to this feast, for My time has not yet fully come." ⁹When He had said these things to them, He remained in Galilee.

84. Jesus Explains Real Greatness

Lk 9:46 ⁴⁶Then a dispute arose among them as to which of them would be greatest.

Matt 18:1 ¹At that time the disciples came to Jesus, saying, "Who then is greatest in the kingdom of heaven?"

Mk 9:33–36 ³³Then He came to Capernaum. And when He was in the house He asked them, "What was it you disputed among yourselves on the road?" ³⁴But they kept silent, for on the road they had disputed among themselves who would be the greatest. ³⁵And He sat down, called the twelve, and said to them, "If anyone desires to be first, he shall be last of all and servant of all." ³⁶Then He took a little child and set him in the midst of them. And [took] him in His arms.

Matt 18:3–4 ³"Assuredly, I say to you, unless you are converted and become as little children, you will by no means enter the kingdom of heaven. ⁴Therefore whoever humbles himself as this little child is the greatest in the kingdom of heaven."

Lk 9:48 ⁴⁸"Whoever receives this little child in My

name receives Me; and whoever receives Me receives Him who sent Me. For he who is least among you all will be great."

Mk 9:38-41 [38]Now John answered Him, saying, "Teacher, we saw someone who does not follow us casting out demons in Your name, and we forbade him because he does not follow us."

[39]But Jesus said, "Do not forbid him, for no one who works a miracle in My name can soon afterward speak evil of Me. [40]For he who is not against us is on our side. [41]For whoever gives you a cup of water to drink in My name, because you belong to Christ, assuredly, I say to you, he will by no means lose his reward."

Matt 18:6-10 [6]"But whoever causes one of these little ones who believe in Me to sin, it would be better for him if a millstone were hung around his neck, and he were drowned in the depth of the sea. [7]Woe to the world because of offenses! For offenses must come, but woe to that man by whom the offense comes!

[8]"If your hand or foot causes you to sin, cut it off and cast it from you. It is better for you to enter into life lame or maimed, rather than having two hands or two feet, to be cast into the everlasting fire. [9]And if your eye causes you to sin, pluck it out and cast it from you. It is better for you to enter into life with one eye, rather than having two eyes, to be cast into hell fire.

[10]"Take heed that you do not despise one of these little ones, for I say to you that in heaven their

angels always see the face of My Father who is in heaven."

Mk 9:48-50 ⁴⁸"Where

> 'Their worm does not die
> And the fire is not quenched.'

⁴⁹"For everyone will be seasoned with fire, and every sacrifice will be seasoned with salt. ⁵⁰Salt is good, but if the salt loses its flavor, how will you season it? Have salt in yourselves, and have peace with one another."

Matt 18:10-35 ¹⁰"Take heed that you do not despise one of these little ones, for I say to you that in heaven their angels always see the face of My Father who is in heaven. ¹¹For the Son of Man has come to save that which was lost.

¹²"What do you think? If a man has a hundred sheep, and one of them goes astray, does he not leave the ninety-nine and go to the mountains to seek the one that is straying? ¹³And if he should find it, assuredly, I say to you, he rejoices more over that sheep than over the ninety-nine that did not go astray. ¹⁴Even so it is not the will of your Father who is in heaven that one of these little ones should perish.

¹⁵"Moreover if your brother sins against you, go and tell him his fault between you and him alone. If he hears you, you have gained your brother. ¹⁶But if he will not hear, take with you one or two more, that 'by the mouth of two or three

witnesses every word may be established.' ¹⁷And if he refuses to hear them, tell it to the church. But if he refuses even to hear the church, let him be to you like a heathen and a tax collector.

¹⁸"Assuredly, I say to you, whatever you bind on earth will be bound in heaven, and whatever you loose on earth will be loosed in heaven.

¹⁹"Again I say to you that if two of you agree on earth concerning anything that they ask, it will be done for them by My Father in heaven. ²⁰For where two or three are gathered together in My name, I am there in the midst of them."

²¹Then Peter came to Him and said, "Lord, how often shall my brother sin against me, and I forgive him? Up to seven times?"

²²Jesus said to him, "I do not say to you, up to seven times, but up to seventy times seven. ²³Therefore the kingdom of heaven is like a certain king who wanted to settle accounts with his servants. ²⁴And when he had begun to settle accounts, one was brought to him who owed him ten thousand talents. ²⁵But as he was not able to pay, his master commanded that he be sold, with his wife and children and all that he had, and that payment be made. ²⁶The servant therefore fell down before him, saying, 'Master, have patience with me, and I will pay you all.' ²⁷Then the master of that servant was moved with compassion, released him, and forgave him the debt.

²⁸"But that servant went out and found one of his fellow servants who owed him a hundred

denarii; and he laid hands on him and took him by the throat, saying, 'Pay me what you owe!' ²⁹So his fellow servant fell down at his feet and begged him, saying, 'Have patience with me, and I will pay you all.' ³⁰And he would not, but went and threw him into prison till he should pay the debt. ³¹So when his fellow servants saw what had been done, they were very grieved, and came and told their master all that had been done. ³²Then his master, after he had called him, said to him, 'You wicked servant! I forgave you all that debt because you begged me. ³³Should you not also have had compassion on your fellow servant, just as I had pity on you?' ³⁴And his master was angry, and delivered him to the torturers until he should pay all that was due to him.

³⁵"So My heavenly Father also will do to you if each of you, from his heart, does not forgive his brother his trespasses."

85. Samaritans Are Unfriendly to Jesus

Lk 9:51 ⁵¹Now it came to pass, when the time had come for Him to be received up, that He steadfastly set His face to go to Jerusalem.

Jn 7:10 ¹⁰But when His brothers had gone up, then He also went up to the feast, not openly, but as it were in secret.

Lk 9:52-56 ⁵²[He] sent messengers before His face. And as they went, they entered a village of the Samaritans, to prepare for Him. ⁵³But they did not receive Him, because His face was set for the journey to Jerusalem. ⁵⁴And when His disciples James and John saw this, they said, "Lord, do You want us to command fire to come down from heaven and consume them, just as Elijah did?"

⁵⁵But He turned and rebuked them, and said, "You do not know what manner of spirit you are of. ⁵⁶For the Son of Man did not come to destroy men's lives but to save them." And they went to another village.

86. Meaning Well Is Not Enough

Lk 9:57–62 ⁵⁷Now it happened as they journeyed on the road, that someone said to Him, "Lord, I will follow You wherever You go."

⁵⁸And Jesus said to him, "Foxes have holes and birds of the air have nests, but the Son of Man has nowhere to lay His head."

⁵⁹Then He said to another, "Follow Me."

But he said, "Lord, let me first go and bury my father."

⁶⁰Jesus said to him, "Let the dead bury their own dead, but you go and preach the kingdom of God."

⁶¹And another also said, "Lord, I will follow You, but let me first go and bid them farewell who are at my house."

⁶²But Jesus said to him, "No one, having put his hand to the plow, and looking back, is fit for the kingdom of God."

JESUS RETURNS TO JUDEA AT FEAST OF TABERNACLES

87. Jesus Makes an Appearance

Jn 7:11-53 ¹¹Then the Jews sought Him at the feast, and said, "Where is He?" ¹²And there was much complaining among the people concerning Him. Some said, "He is good"; others said, "No, on the contrary, He deceives the people." ¹³However, no one spoke openly of Him for fear of the Jews.

¹⁴Now about the middle of the feast Jesus went up into the temple and taught. ¹⁵And the Jews marveled, saying, "How does this Man know letters, having never studied?"

¹⁶Jesus answered them and said, "My doctrine is not Mine, but His who sent Me. ¹⁷If anyone wills to do His will, he shall know concerning the doctrine, whether it is from God or whether I speak on My own authority. ¹⁸He who speaks from himself seeks his own glory; but He who seeks the glory of

the One who sent Him is true, and no unrighteousness is in Him. ¹⁹Did not Moses give you the law, yet none of you keeps the law? Why do you seek to kill Me?"

²⁰The people answered and said, "You have a demon. Who is seeking to kill You?"

²¹Jesus answered and said to them, "I did one work, and you all marvel. ²²Moses therefore gave you circumcision (not that it is from Moses, but from the fathers), and you circumcise a man on the Sabbath. ²³If a man receives circumcision on the Sabbath, so that the law of Moses should not be broken, are you angry with Me because I made a man completely well on the Sabbath? ²⁴Do not judge according to appearance, but judge with righteous judgment."

²⁵Now some of them from Jerusalem said, "Is this not He whom they seek to kill? ²⁶But look! He speaks boldly, and they say nothing to Him. Do the rulers know indeed that this is truly the Christ? ²⁷However, we know where this Man is from; but when the Christ comes, no one knows where He is from."

²⁸Then Jesus cried out, as He taught in the temple, saying, "You both know Me, and you know where I am from; and I have not come of Myself, but He who sent Me is true, whom you do not know. ²⁹But I know Him, for I am from Him, and He sent Me."

³⁰Therefore they sought to take Him; but no one laid a hand on Him, because His hour had not

yet come. ³¹And many of the people believed in I Him, and said, "When the Christ comes, will He do more signs than these which this Man has done?"

³²The Pharisees heard the crowd murmuring these things concerning Him, and the Pharisees and the chief priests sent officers to take Him. ³³Then Jesus said to them, "I shall be with you a little while longer, and then I go to Him who sent Me. ³⁴You will seek Me and not find Me, and where I am you cannot come."

³⁵Then the Jews said among themselves, "Where does He intend to go that we shall not find Him? Does He intend to go to the Dispersion among the Greeks and teach the Greeks? ³⁶What is this thing that He said, 'You will seek Me and not find Me, and where I am you cannot come'?"

³⁷On the last day, that great day of the feast, Jesus stood and cried out, saying, "If anyone thirsts, let him come to Me and drink. ³⁸He who believes in Me, as the Scripture has said, out of his heart will flow rivers of living water." ³⁹But this He spoke concerning the Spirit, whom those believing in Him would receive; for the Holy Spirit was not yet given, because Jesus was not yet glorified.

⁴⁰Therefore many from the crowd, when they heard this saying, said, "Truly this is the Prophet." ⁴¹Others said, "This is the Christ."

But some said, "Will the Christ come out of Galilee? ⁴²Has not the Scripture said that the Christ comes from the seed of David and from the town of Bethlehem, where David was?" ⁴³So there was a division among the people because of Him. ⁴⁴Now some of them wanted to take Him, but no one laid hands on Him.

⁴⁵Then the officers came to the chief priests and Pharisees, who said to them, "Why have you not brought Him?"

⁴⁶The officers answered, "No man ever spoke like this Man!"

⁴⁷Then the Pharisees answered them, "Are you also deceived? ⁴⁸Have any of the rulers or the Pharisees believed in Him? ⁴⁹But this crowd that does not know the law is accursed."

⁵⁰Nicodemus (he who came to Jesus by night, being one of them) said to them, ⁵¹"Does our law judge a man before it hears him and knows what he is doing?"

⁵²They answered and said to him, "Are you also from Galilee? Search and look, for no prophet has arisen out of Galilee."

⁵³And everyone went to his own house.

88. The Savior Forgives an Adultery Victim

Jn 8:1-11 ¹But Jesus went to the Mount of Olives.
²Now early in the morning He came again into the temple, and all the people came to Him; and He sat down and taught them. ³Then the scribes and Pharisees brought to Him a woman caught in adultery. And when they had set her in the midst, ⁴they said to Him, "Teacher, this woman was caught in adultery, in the very act. ⁵Now Moses, in

the law, commanded us that such should be stoned. But what do You say?" ⁶This they said, testing Him, that they might have something of which to accuse Him. But Jesus stooped down and wrote on the ground with His finger, as though He did not hear.

⁷So when they continued asking Him, He raised Himself up and said to them, "He who is without sin among you, let him throw a stone at her first." ⁸And again He stooped down and wrote on the ground. ⁹Then those who heard it, being convicted by their conscience, went out one by one, beginning with the oldest even to the last. And Jesus was left alone, and the woman standing in the midst. ¹⁰When Jesus had raised Himself up and saw no one but the woman, He said to her, "Woman, where are those accusers of yours? Has no one condemned you?"

¹¹She said, "No one, Lord."

And Jesus said to her, "Neither do I condemn you; go and sin no more."

89. Jews Attack the Master

Jn 8:12–59 ¹²Then Jesus spoke to them again, saying, "I am the light of the world. He who follows Me shall not walk in darkness, but have the light of life."

¹³The Pharisees therefore said to Him, "You bear witness of Yourself; Your witness is not true."

¹⁴Jesus answered and said to them, "Even if I bear witness of Myself, My witness is true, for I know where I came from and where I am going;

but you do not know where I come from and where I am going. ¹⁵You judge according to the flesh; I judge no one. ¹⁶And yet if I do judge, My judgment is true; for I am not alone, but I am with the Father who sent Me. ¹⁷It is also written in your law that the testimony of two men is true. ¹⁸I am One who bears witness of Myself, and the Father who sent Me bears witness of Me."

¹⁹Then they said to Him, "Where is Your Father?"

Jesus answered, "You know neither Me nor My Father. If you had known Me, you would have known My Father also."

²⁰These words Jesus spoke in the treasury, as He taught in the temple; and no one laid hands on Him, for His hour had not yet come.

²¹Then Jesus said to them again, "I am going away, and you will seek Me, and will die in your sin. Where I go you cannot come."

²²So the Jews said, "Will He kill Himself, because He says, 'Where I go you cannot come'?"

²³And He said to them, "You are from beneath; I am from above. You are of this world; I am not of this world. ²⁴Therefore I said to you that you will die in your sins; for if you do not believe that I am He, you will die in your sins."

²⁵Then they said to Him, "Who are You?"

And Jesus said to them, "Just what I have been saying to you from the beginning. ²⁶I have many things to say and to judge concerning you, but He who sent Me is true, and I speak to the world those things which I heard from Him."

²⁷They did not understand that He spoke to them of the Father.

²⁸Then Jesus said to them, "When you lift up the Son of Man, then you will know that I am He, and that I do nothing of Myself; but as My Father taught Me, I speak these things. ²⁹And He who sent Me is with Me. The Father has not left Me alone, for I always do those things that please Him." ³⁰As He spoke these words, many believed in Him.

³¹Then Jesus said to those Jews who believed Him, "If you abide in My word, you are My disciples indeed. ³²And you shall know the truth, and the truth shall make you free."

³³They answered Him, "We are Abraham's descendants, and have never been in bondage to anyone. How can You say, 'You will be made free'?"

³⁴Jesus answered them, "Most assuredly, I say to you, whoever commits sin is a slave of sin. ³⁵And a slave does not abide in the house forever, but a son abides forever. ³⁶Therefore if the Son makes you free, you shall be free indeed.

³⁷"I know that you are Abraham's descendants, but you seek to kill Me, because My word has no place in you. ³⁸I speak what I have seen with My Father, and you do what you have seen with your father."

³⁹They answered and said to Him, "Abraham is our father."

Jesus said to them, "If you were Abraham's children, you would do the works of Abraham. ⁴⁰But now you seek to kill Me, a Man who has told you the truth which I heard from God. Abraham did not do this. ⁴¹You do the deeds of your father."

Then they said to Him, "We were not born of fornication; we have one Father—God."

⁴²Jesus said to them, "If God were your Father, you would love Me, for I proceeded forth and came from God; nor have I come of Myself, but He sent Me. ⁴³Why do you not understand My speech? Because you are not able to listen to My word. ⁴⁴You are of your father the devil, and the desires of your father you want to do. He was a murderer from the beginning, and does not stand in the truth, because there is no truth in him. When he speaks a lie, he speaks from his own resources, for he is a liar and the father of it. ⁴⁵But because I tell the truth, you do not believe Me. ⁴⁶Which of you convicts Me of sin? And if I tell the truth, why do you not believe Me? ⁴⁷He who is of God hears God's words; therefore you do not hear, because you are not of God."

⁴⁸Then the Jews answered and said to Him, "Do we not say rightly that You are a Samaritan and have a demon?"

⁴⁹Jesus answered, "I do not have a demon; but I honor My Father, and you dishonor Me. ⁵⁰And I do not seek My own glory; there is One who seeks and judges. ⁵¹Most assuredly, I say to you, if anyone keeps My word he shall never see death."

⁵²Then the Jews said to Him, "Now we know that You have a demon! Abraham is dead, and the prophets; and You say, 'If anyone keeps My word he shall never taste death.' ⁵³Are You greater than our father Abraham, who is dead? And the prophets are dead. Who do You make Yourself out to be?"

⁵⁴Jesus answered, "If I honor Myself, My honor is nothing. It is My Father who honors Me, of whom you say that He is your God. ⁵⁵Yet you have not known Him, but I know Him. And if I say, 'I do not know Him,' I shall be a liar like you; but I do know Him and keep His word. ⁵⁶Your father Abraham rejoiced to see My day, and he saw it and was glad."

⁵⁷Then the Jews said to Him, "You are not yet fifty years old, and have You seen Abraham?"

⁵⁸Jesus said to them, "Most assuredly, I say to you, before Abraham was, I AM."

⁵⁹Then they took up stones to throw at Him; but Jesus hid Himself and went out of the temple, going through the midst of them, and so passed by.

90. Man Sees for the First Time

Jn 9:1-41 ¹Now as Jesus passed by, He saw a man who was blind from birth. ²And His disciples asked Him, saying, "Rabbi, who sinned, this man or his parents, that he was born blind?"

³Jesus answered, "Neither this man nor his parents sinned, but that the works of God should

be revealed in him. ⁴I must work the works of Him who sent Me while it is day; the night is coming when no one can work. ⁵As long as I am in the world, I am the light of the world."

⁶When He had said these things, He spat on the ground and made clay with the saliva; and He anointed the eyes of the blind man with the clay. ⁷And He said to him, "Go, wash in the pool of Siloam" (which is translated, Sent). So he went and washed, and came back seeing.

⁸Therefore the neighbors and those who previously had seen that he was blind said, "Is not this he who sat and begged?"

⁹Some said, "This is he." Others said, "He is like him."

He said, "I am he."

¹⁰Therefore they said to him, "How were your eyes opened?"

¹¹He answered and said, "A Man called Jesus made clay and anointed my eyes and said to me, 'Go to the pool of Siloam and wash.' So I went and washed, and I received sight."

¹²Then they said to him, "Where is He?"

He said, "I do not know."

¹³They brought him who formerly was blind to the Pharisees. ¹⁴Now it was a Sabbath when Jesus made the clay and opened his eyes. ¹⁵Then the Pharisees also asked him again how he had received his sight. He said to them, "He put clay on my eyes, and I washed, and I see."

¹⁶Therefore some of the Pharisees said, "This

Man is not from God, because He does not keep the Sabbath."

Others said, "How can a man who is a sinner do such signs?" And there was a division among them.

[17]They said to the blind man again, "What do you say about Him because He opened your eyes?"

He said, "He is a prophet."

[18]But the Jews did not believe concerning him, that he had been blind and received his sight, until they called the parents of him who had received his sight. [19]And they asked them, saying, "Is this your son, who you say was born blind? How then does he now see?"

[20]His parents answered them and said, "We know that this is our son, and that he was born blind; [21]but by what means he now sees we do not know, or who opened his eyes we do not know. He is of age; ask him. He will speak for himself." [22]His parents said these things because they feared the Jews, for the Jews had agreed already that if anyone confessed that He was Christ, he would be put out of the synagogue. [23]Therefore his parents said, "He is of age; ask him."

[24]So they again called the man who was blind, and said to him, "Give God the glory! We know that this Man is a sinner."

[25]He answered and said, "Whether He is a sinner or not I do not know. One thing I know: that though I was blind, now I see."

²⁶Then they said to him again, "What did He do to you? How did He open your eyes?"

²⁷He answered them, "I told you already, and you did not listen. Why do you want to hear it again? Do you also want to become His disciples?"

²⁸Then they reviled him and said, "You are His disciple, but we are Moses' disciples. ²⁹We know that God spoke to Moses; as for this fellow, we do not know where He is from."

³⁰The man answered and said to them, "Why, this is a marvelous thing, that you do not know where He is from; yet He has opened my eyes! ³¹Now we know that God does not hear sinners; but if anyone is a worshiper of God and does His will, He hears him. ³²Since the world began it has been unheard of that anyone opened the eyes of one who was born blind. ³³If this Man were not from God, He could do nothing."

³⁴They answered and said to him, "You were completely born in sins, and are you teaching us?" And they cast him out.

³⁵Jesus heard that they had cast him out; and when He had found him, He said to him, "Do you believe in the Son of God?"

³⁶He answered and said, "Who is He, Lord, that I may believe in Him?"

³⁷And Jesus said to him, "You have both seen Him and it is He who is talking with you."

³⁸Then he said, "Lord, I believe!" And he worshiped Him.

³⁹And Jesus said, "For judgment I have come into this world, that those who do not see may see, and that those who see may be made blind."

⁴⁰Then some of the Pharisees who were with Him heard these words, and said to Him, "Are we blind also?"

⁴¹Jesus said to them, "If you were blind, you would have no sin; but now you say, 'We see.' Therefore your sin remains."

91. Jesus as Shepherd

Jn 10:1–21 ¹"Most assuredly, I say to you, he who does not enter the sheepfold by the door, but climbs up some other way, the same is a thief and a robber. ²But he who enters by the door is the shepherd of the sheep. ³To him the doorkeeper opens, and the sheep hear his voice; and he calls his own sheep by name and leads them out. ⁴And when he brings out his own sheep, he goes before them; and the sheep follow him, for they know his voice. ⁵Yet they will by no means follow a stranger, but will flee from him, for they do not know the voice of strangers." ⁶Jesus used this illustration, but they did not understand the things which He spoke to them.

⁷Then Jesus said to them again, "Most assuredly, I say to you, I am the door of the sheep. ⁸All who ever came before Me are thieves and robbers, but the sheep did not hear them. ⁹I am the door. If anyone enters by Me, he will be saved, and

will go in and out and find pasture. ¹⁰The thief does not come except to steal, and to kill, and to destroy. I have come that they may have life, and that they may have it more abundantly.

¹¹"I am the good shepherd. The good shepherd gives His life for the sheep. ¹²But a hireling, he who is not the shepherd, one who does not own the sheep, sees the wolf coming and leaves the sheep and flees; and the wolf catches the sheep and scatters them. ¹³The hireling flees because he is a hireling and does not care about the sheep. ¹⁴I am the good shepherd; and I know My sheep, and am known by My own. ¹⁵As the Father knows Me, even so I know the Father; and I lay down My life for the sheep. ¹⁶And other sheep I have which are not of this fold; them also I must bring, and they will hear My voice; and there will be one flock and one shepherd.

¹⁷"Therefore My Father loves Me, because I lay down My life that I may take it again. ¹⁸No one takes it from Me, but I lay it down of Myself. I have power to lay it down, and I have power to take it again. This command I have received from My Father."

¹⁹Therefore there was a division again among the Jews because of these sayings. ²⁰And many of them said, "He has a demon and is mad. Why do you listen to Him?"

²¹Others said, "These are not the words of one who has a demon. Can a demon open the eyes of the blind?"

92. Evangelism in Pairs: Jesus Sends Seventy

Lk 10:1-24 ¹After these things the Lord appointed seventy others also, and sent them two by two before His face into every city and place where He Himself was about to go. ²Then He said to them, "The harvest truly is great, but the laborers are few; therefore pray the Lord of the harvest to send out laborers into His harvest. ³Go your way; behold, I send you out as lambs among wolves. ⁴Carry neither money bag, knapsack, nor sandals; and greet no one along the road. ⁵But whatever house you enter, first say, 'Peace to this house.' ⁶And if a son of peace is there, your peace will rest on it; if not, it will return to you. ⁷And remain in the same house, eating and drinking such things as they give, for the laborer is worthy of his wages. Do not go from house to house. ⁸Whatever city you enter, and they receive you, eat such things as are set before you. ⁹And heal the sick there, and say to them, 'The kingdom of God has come near to you.' ¹⁰But whatever city you enter, and they do not receive you, go out into its streets and say, ¹¹'The very dust of your city which clings to us we wipe off against you. Nevertheless know this, that the kingdom of God has come near you.' ¹²But I say to you that it will be more tolerable in that Day for Sodom than for that city.

¹³"Woe to you, Chorazin! Woe to you, Bethsaida! For if the mighty works which were

done in you had been done in Tyre and Sidon, they would have repented long ago, sitting in sackcloth and ashes. ¹⁴But it will be more tolerable for Tyre and Sidon at the judgment than for you. ¹⁵And you, Capernaum, who are exalted to heaven, will be brought down to Hades. ¹⁶He who hears you hears Me, he who rejects you rejects Me, and he who rejects Me rejects Him who sent Me."

¹⁷Then the seventy returned with joy, saying, "Lord, even the demons are subject to us in Your name."

¹⁸And He said to them, "I saw Satan fall like lightning from heaven. ¹⁹Behold, I give you the authority to trample on serpents and scorpions, and over all the power of the enemy, and nothing shall by any means hurt you. ²⁰Nevertheless do not rejoice in this, that the spirits are subject to you, but rather rejoice because your names are written in heaven."

²¹In that hour Jesus rejoiced in the Spirit and said, "I thank You, Father, Lord of heaven and earth, that You have hidden these things from the wise and prudent and revealed them to babes. Even so, Father, for so it seemed good in Your sight. ²²All things have been delivered to Me by My Father, and no one knows who the Son is except the Father, and who the Father is except the Son, and the one to whom the Son wills to reveal Him."

²³Then He turned to His disciples and said privately, "Blessed are the eyes which see the things you see; ²⁴for I tell you that many prophets

and kings have desired to see what you see, and
have not seen it, and to hear what you hear, and
have not heard it."

93. Samaritan Shows True Colors

Lk 10:25-37 ²⁵And behold, a certain lawyer stood
up and tested Him, saying, "Teacher, what shall I
do to inherit eternal life?"

²⁶He said to him, "What is written in the law?
What is your reading of it?"

²⁷So he answered and said, "'You shall love the
LORD your God with all your heart, with all your
soul, with all your strength, and with all your mind,'
and 'your neighbor as yourself.'"

²⁸And He said to him, "You have answered
rightly; do this and you will live."

²⁹But he, wanting to justify himself, said to
Jesus, "And who is my neighbor?"

³⁰Then Jesus answered and said: "A certain
man went down from Jerusalem to Jericho, and fell
among thieves, who stripped him of his clothing,
wounded him, and departed, leaving him half dead.
³¹Now by chance a certain priest came down that
road. And when he saw him, he passed by on the
other side. ³²Likewise a Levite, when he arrived at
the place, came and looked, and passed by on the
other side. ³³But a certain Samaritan, as he journeyed, came where he was. And when he saw him,
he had compassion. ³⁴So he went to him and
bandaged his wounds, pouring on oil and wine;
and he set him on his own animal, brought him to

an inn, and took care of him. ³⁵On the next day, when he departed, he took out two denarii, gave them to the innkeeper, and said to him, 'Take care of him; and whatever more you spend, when I come again, I will repay you.' ³⁶So which of these three do you think was neighbor to him who fell among the thieves?"

³⁷And he said, "He who showed mercy on him."

Then Jesus said to him, "Go and do likewise."

94. *Mary and Martha Entertain Jesus*

Lk 10:38–42 ³⁸Now it happened as they went that He entered a certain village; and a certain woman named Martha welcomed Him into her house. ³⁹And she had a sister called Mary, who also sat at Jesus' feet and heard His word. ⁴⁰But Martha was distracted with much serving, and she approached Him and said, "Lord, do You not care that my sister has left me to serve alone? Therefore tell her to help me."

⁴¹And Jesus answered and said to her, "Martha, Martha, you are worried and troubled about many things. ⁴²But one thing is needed, and Mary has chosen that good part, which will not be taken away from her."

95. *How One Should Pray*

Lk 11:1–13 ¹Now it came to pass, as He was pray-ing in a certain place, when He ceased, that one of

His disciples said to Him, "Lord, teach us to pray, as John also taught his disciples.

²So He said to them, "When you pray, say:

>   Our Father in heaven,
>   Hallowed be Your name.
>   Your kingdom come.
>   Your will be done
>   On earth as it is in heaven.
> ³   Give us day by day our daily bread.
> ⁴   And forgive us our sins,
>   For we also forgive everyone who is
>   indebted to us.
>   And do not lead us into temptation,
>   But deliver us from the evil one."

⁵And He said to them, "Which of you shall have a friend, and go to him at midnight and say to him, 'Friend, lend me three loaves; ⁶for a friend of mine has come to me on his journey, and I have nothing to set before him'; ⁷and he will answer from within and say, 'Do not trouble me; the door is now shut, and my children are with me in bed; I cannot rise and give to you'? ⁸I say to you, though he will not rise and give to him because he is his friend, yet because of his persistence he will rise and give him as many as he needs.

⁹"So I say to you, ask, and it will be given to you; seek, and you will find; knock, and it will be opened to you. ¹⁰For everyone who asks receives, and he who seeks finds, and to him who knocks it

will be opened. ¹¹If a son asks for bread from any father among you, will he give him a stone? Or if he asks for a fish, will he give him a serpent instead of a fish? ¹²Or if he asks for an egg, will he offer him a scorpion? ¹³If you then, being evil, know how to give good gifts to your children, how much more will your heavenly Father give the Holy Spirit to those who ask Him!"

96. Demon Releases a Mute

Lk 11:14-36 ¹⁴And He was casting out a demon, and it was mute. So it was, when the demon had gone out, that the mute spoke; and the multitudes marveled. ¹⁵But some of them said, "He casts out demons by Beelzebub, the ruler of the demons."

¹⁶Others, testing Him, sought from Him a sign from heaven. ¹⁷But He, knowing their thoughts, said to them: "Every kingdom divided against itself is brought to desolation, and a house divided against a house falls. ¹⁸If Satan also is divided against himself, how will his kingdom stand? Because you say I cast out demons by Beelzebub. ¹⁹And if I cast out demons by Beelzebub, by whom do your sons cast them out? Therefore they will be your judges. ²⁰But if I cast out demons with the finger of God, surely the kingdom of God has come upon you. ²¹When a strong man, fully armed, guards his own palace, his goods are in peace. ²²But when a stronger than he comes upon him and overcomes him, he takes from him all his armor in which he trusted, and divides his spoils.

²³He who is not with Me is against Me, and he who does not gather with Me scatters.

²⁴"When an unclean spirit goes out of a man, he goes through dry places, seeking rest; and finding none, he says, 'I will return to my house from which I came.' ²⁵And when he comes, he finds it swept and put in order. ²⁶Then he goes and takes with him seven other spirits more wicked than himself, and they enter and dwell there; and the last state of that man is worse than the first."

²⁷And it happened, as He spoke these things, that a certain woman from the crowd raised her voice and said to Him, "Blessed is the womb that bore You, and the breasts which nursed You!"

²⁸But He said, "More than that, blessed are those who hear the word of God and keep it!"

²⁹And while the crowds were thickly gathered together, He began to say, "This is an evil generation. It seeks a sign, and no sign will be given to it except the sign of Jonah the prophet. ³⁰For as Jonah became a sign to the Ninevites, so also the Son of Man will be to this generation. ³¹The queen of the South will rise up in the judgment with the men of this generation and condemn them, for she came from the ends of the earth to hear the wisdom of Solomon; and indeed a greater than Solomon is here. ³²The men of Nineveh will rise up in the judgment with this generation and condemn it, for they repented at the preaching of Jonah; and indeed a greater than Jonah is here.

³³"No one, when he has lit a lamp, puts it in a secret place or under a basket, but on a lampstand, that those who come in may see the light. ³⁴The lamp of the body is the eye. Therefore, when your eye is good, your whole body also is full of light. But when your eye is bad, your body also is full of darkness. ³⁵Therefore take heed that the light which is in you is not darkness. ³⁶If then your whole body is full of light, having no part dark, the whole body will be full of light, as when the bright shining of a lamp gives you light."

97. Jesus Advocates Genuine Sincerity

Lk 11:37-53 ³⁷And as He spoke, a certain Pharisee asked Him to dine with him. So He went in and sat down to eat. ³⁸When the Pharisee saw it, he marveled that He had not first washed before dinner.

³⁹Then the Lord said to him, "Now you Pharisees make the outside of the cup and dish clean, but your inward part is full of greed and wickedness. ⁴⁰Foolish ones! Did not He who made the outside make the inside also? ⁴¹But rather give alms of such things as you have; then indeed all things are clean to you.

⁴²"But woe to you Pharisees! For you tithe mint and rue and all manner of herbs, and pass by justice and the love of God. These you ought to have done, without leaving the others undone. ⁴³Woe to you Pharisees! For you love the best seats in the synagogues and greetings in the marketplaces.

⁴⁴"Woe to you, scribes and Pharisees, hypocrites! For you are like graves which are not seen, and the men who walk over them are not aware of them."

⁴⁵Then one of the lawyers answered and said to Him, "Teacher, by saying these things You reproach us also."

⁴⁶And He said, "Woe to you also, lawyers! For you load men with burdens hard to bear, and you yourselves do not touch the burdens with one of your fingers. ⁴⁷Woe to you! For you build the tombs of the prophets, and your fathers killed them. ⁴⁸In fact, you bear witness that you approve the deeds of your fathers; for they indeed killed them, and you build their tombs. ⁴⁹Therefore the wisdom of God also said, 'I will send them prophets and apostles, and some of them they will kill and persecute,' ⁵⁰that the blood of all the prophets which was shed from the foundation of the world may be required of this generation, ⁵¹from the blood of Abel to the blood of Zechariah who perished between the altar and the temple. Yes, I say to you, it shall be required of this generation.

⁵²"Woe to you lawyers! For you have taken away the key of knowledge. You did not enter in yourselves, and those who were entering in you hindered."

⁵³And as He said these things to them, the scribes and the Pharisees began to assail Him vehemently, and to cross-examine Him about many things.

98. Pharisees Are Not Genuine

Lk 12:1-3 ¹In the meantime, when an innumerable multitude of people had gathered together, so that they trampled one another, He began to say to His disciples first of all, "Beware of the leaven of the Pharisees, which is hypocrisy. ²For there is nothing covered that will not be revealed, nor hidden that will not be known. ³Therefore whatever you have spoken in the dark will be heard in the light, and what you have spoken in the ear in inner rooms will be proclaimed on the housetops."

99. Hope for Real Followers

Lk 12:4-12 ⁴"And I say to you, My friends, do not be afraid of those who kill the body, and after that have no more that they can do. ⁵But I will show you whom you should fear: Fear Him who, after He has killed, has power to cast into hell; yes, I say to you, fear Him!

⁶"Are not five sparrows sold for two copper coins? And not one of them is forgotten before God. ⁷But the very hairs of your head are all numbered. Do not fear therefore; you are of more value than many sparrows.

⁸"Also I say to you, whoever confesses Me before men, him the Son of Man also will confess before the angels of God. ⁹But he who denies Me before men will be denied before the angels of God.

¹⁰"And anyone who speaks a word against the Son of Man, it will be forgiven him; but to him who blasphemes against the Holy Spirit, it will not be forgiven.

¹¹"Now when they bring you to the synagogues and magistrates and authorities, do not worry about how or what you should answer, or what you should say. ¹²For the Holy Spirit will teach you in that very hour what you ought to say."

100. Lessons from the Master Teacher

Lk 12:13–59 ¹³Then one from the crowd said to Him, "Teacher, tell my brother to divide the inheritance with me."

¹⁴But He said to him, "Man, who made Me a judge or an arbitrator over you?" ¹⁵And He said to them, "Take heed and beware of covetousness, for one's life does not consist in the abundance of the things he possesses."

¹⁶Then He spoke a parable to them, saying: "The ground of a certain rich man yielded plentifully. ¹⁷And he thought within himself, saying, 'What shall I do, since I have no room to store my crops?' ¹⁸So he said, 'I will do this: I will pull down my barns and build greater, and there I will store all my crops and my goods. ¹⁹And I will say to my soul, "Soul, you have many goods laid up for many years; take your ease; eat, drink, and be merry."' ²⁰But God said to him, 'Fool! This night your soul will be required of you; then whose will those things be which you have provided?'

²¹"So is he who lays up treasure for himself, and is not rich toward God."

²²Then He said to His disciples, "Therefore I say to you, do not worry about your life, what you will eat; nor about the body, what you will put on. ²³Life is more than food, and the body is more than clothing. ²⁴Consider the ravens, for they neither sow nor reap, which have neither storehouse nor barn; and God feeds them. Of how much more value are you than the birds? ²⁵And which of you by worrying can add one cubit to his stature? ²⁶If you then are not able to do the least, why are you anxious for the rest? ²⁷Consider the lilies, how they grow: they neither toil nor spin; and yet I say to you, even Solomon in all his glory was not arrayed like one of these. ²⁸If then God so clothes the grass, which today is in the field and tomorrow is thrown into the oven, how much more will He clothe you, O you of little faith?

²⁹"And do not seek what you should eat or what you should drink, nor have an anxious mind. ³⁰For all these things the nations of the world seek after, and your Father knows that you need these things. ³¹But seek the kingdom of God, and all these things shall be added to you.

³²"Do not fear, little flock, for it is your Father's good pleasure to give you the kingdom. ³³Sell what you have and give alms; provide yourselves money bags which do not grow old, a treasure in the heavens that does not fail, where no thief approaches nor moth destroys.

³⁴For where your treasure is, there your heart will be also.

³⁵"Let your waist be girded and your lamps burning; ³⁶and you yourselves be like men who wait for their master, when he will return from the wedding, that when he comes and knocks they may open to him immediately. ³⁷Blessed are those servants whom the master, when he comes, will find watching. Assuredly, I say to you that he will gird himself and have them sit down to eat, and will come and serve them. ³⁸And if he should come in the second watch, or come in the third watch, and find them so, blessed are those servants. ³⁹But know this, that if the master of the house had known what hour the thief would come, he would have watched and not allowed his house to be broken into. ⁴⁰Therefore you also be ready, for the Son of Man is coming at an hour you do not expect."

⁴¹Then Peter said to Him, "Lord, do You speak this parable only to us, or to all people?"

⁴²And the Lord said, "Who then is that faithful and wise steward, whom his master will make ruler over his household, to give them their portion of food in due season? ⁴³Blessed is that servant whom his master will find so doing when he comes. ⁴⁴Truly, I say to you that he will make him ruler over all that he has. ⁴⁵But if that servant says in his heart, 'My master is delaying his coming,' and begins to beat the male and female servants, and to eat and drink and be drunk, ⁴⁶the master of that servant will

come on a day when he is not looking for him, and at an hour when he is not aware, and will cut him in two and appoint him his portion with the unbelievers. [47] And that servant who knew his master's will, and did not prepare himself or do according to his will, shall be beaten with many stripes. [48] But he who did not know, yet committed things deserving of stripes, shall be beaten with few. For everyone to whom much is given, from him much will be required; and to whom much has been committed, of him they will ask the more.

[49] "I came to send fire on the earth, and how I wish it were already kindled! [50] But I have a baptism to be baptized with, and how distressed I am till it is accomplished! [51] Do you suppose that I came to give peace on earth? I tell you, not at all, but rather division. [52] For from now on five in one house will be divided: three against two, and two against three. [53] Father will be divided against son and son against father, mother against daughter and daughter against mother, mother-in-law against her daughter-in-law and daughter-in-law against her mother-in-law."

[54] Then He also said to the multitudes, "Whenever you see a cloud rising out of the west, immediately you say, 'A shower is coming'; and so it is. [55] And when you see the south wind blow, you say, 'There will be hot weather'; and there is. [56] Hypocrites! You can discern the face of the sky and of the earth, but how is it you do not discern this time?

⁵⁷"Yes, and why, even of yourselves, do you not judge what is right? ⁵⁸When you go with your adversary to the magistrate, make every effort along the way to settle with him, lest he drag you to the judge, the judge deliver you to the officer, and the officer throw you into prison. ⁵⁹I tell you, you shall not depart from there till you have paid the very last mite."

101. What to Expect from Life's Knocks

Lk 13:1-5 ¹There were present at that season some who told Him about the Galileans whose blood Pilate had mingled with their sacrifices. ²And Jesus answered and said to them, "Do you suppose that these Galileans were worse sinners than all other Galileans, because they suffered such things? ³I tell you, no; but unless you repent you will all likewise perish. ⁴Or those eighteen on whom the tower in Siloam fell and killed them, do you think that they were worse sinners than all other men who dwelt in Jerusalem? ⁵I tell you, no; but unless you repent you will all likewise perish."

102. What God Expects of Us

Lk 13:6-9 ⁶He also spoke this parable: "A certain man had a fig tree planted in his vineyard, and he came seeking fruit on it and found none. ⁷Then he said to the keeper of his vineyard, 'Look, for three years I have come seeking fruit on this fig tree and find none. Cut it down; why does it use up the ground?' ⁸But he answered and said to him, 'Sir, let it alone this year also, until I dig around it and fertilize it. ⁹And if it bears fruit, well. But if not, after that you can cut it down.'"

103. *Jesus Justifies Sabbath Healing*

Lk 13:10–17 ¹⁰Now He was teaching in one of the synagogues on the Sabbath. ¹¹And behold, there was a woman who had a spirit of infirmity eighteen years, and was bent over and could in no way raise herself up. ¹²But when Jesus saw her, He called her to Him and said to her, "Woman, you are loosed from your infirmity." ¹³And He laid His hands on her, and immediately she was made straight, and glorified God.

¹⁴But the ruler of the synagogue answered with indignation, because Jesus had healed on the Sabbath; and he said to the crowd, "There are six days on which men ought to work; therefore come and be healed on them, and not on the Sabbath day."

¹⁵The Lord then answered him and said, "Hypocrite! Does not each one of you on the Sabbath loose his ox or donkey from the stall, and lead it away to water it? ¹⁶So ought not this woman, being a daughter of Abraham, whom Satan has bound—think of it—for eighteen years, be loosed from this bond on the Sabbath?" ¹⁷And when He said these things, all His adversaries were put to shame; and all the multitude rejoiced for all the glorious things that were done by Him.

104. Of Mustard Seed and Leaven

Lk 13:18–21 ¹⁸Then He said, "What is the kingdom of God like? And to what shall I compare it? ¹⁹It is like a mustard seed, which a man took and put in his garden; and it grew and became a large tree, and the birds of the air nested in its branches."

²⁰And again He said, "To what shall I liken the kingdom of God? ²¹It is like leaven, which a woman took and hid in three measures of meal till it was all leavened."

105. The Jews Refuse Jesus

Jn 10:22–39 ²²Now it was the Feast of Dedication in Jerusalem, and it was winter. ²³And Jesus walked in the temple, in Solomon's porch. ²⁴Then the Jews surrounded Him and said to Him, "How long do You keep us in doubt? If You are the Christ, tell us plainly."

²⁵Jesus answered them, "I told you, and you do not believe. The works that I do in My Father's name, they bear witness of Me. ²⁶But you do not believe, because you are not of My sheep, as I said to you. ²⁷My sheep hear My voice, and I know them, and they follow Me. ²⁸And I give them eternal life, and they shall never perish; neither shall anyone snatch them out of My hand. ²⁹My Father, who has given them to Me, is greater than all; and no one is able to snatch them out of My Father's hand. ³⁰I and My Father are one."

³¹Then the Jews took up stones again to stone

Him. [32]Jesus answered them, "Many good works I have shown you from My Father. For which of those works do you stone Me?"

[33]The Jews answered Him, saying, "For a good work we do not stone You, but for blasphemy, and because You, being a Man, make Yourself God."

[34]Jesus answered them, "Is it not written in your law, 'I said, "You are gods"'? [35]If He called them gods, to whom the word of God came (and the Scripture cannot be broken), [36]do you say of Him whom the Father sanctified and sent into the world, 'You are blaspheming,' because I said, 'I am the Son of God'? [37]If I do not do the works of My Father, do not believe Me; [38]but if I do, though you do not believe Me, believe the works, that you may know and believe that the Father is in Me, and I in Him." [39]Therefore they sought again to seize Him, but He escaped out of their hand.

TEACHING BEYOND THE JORDAN RIVER

106. Jesus Among the Pereans

Jn 10:40–42 ⁴⁰And He went away again beyond the Jordan to the place where John was baptizing at first, and there He stayed. ⁴¹Then many came to Him and said, "John performed no sign, but all the things that John spoke about this Man were true." ⁴²And many believed in Him there.

Lk 13:22 ²²And He went through the cities and villages, teaching, and journeying toward Jerusalem.

107. How Many Will Be Saved?

Lk 13:23–30 ²³Then one said to Him, "Lord, are there few who are saved?"

And He said to them, ²⁴"Strive to enter through the narrow gate, for many, I say to you, will seek to enter and will not be able. ²⁵When once the Master of the house has risen up and shut the door, and you begin to stand outside and knock at the door, saying, 'Lord, Lord, open for us,' and He will answer and say to you, 'I do not know you, where you are from,' ²⁶then you will begin to say, 'We ate and drank in Your presence, and You taught in our streets.' ²⁷But He will say, 'I tell you I do not know you, where you are from. Depart from Me, all you workers of iniquity.' ²⁸There will be weeping and gnashing of teeth, when you see Abraham and Isaac and Jacob and all the prophets in the kingdom of God, and yourselves thrust out. ²⁹They will come from the east and the west, from the north and the south, and sit down in the kingdom of God. ³⁰And indeed there are last who will be first, and there are first who will be last."

108. Jesus Confronts Herod Head-On

Lk 13:31-35 ³¹On that very day some Pharisees came, saying to Him, "Get out and depart from here, for Herod wants to kill You."

³²And He said to them, "Go, tell that fox, 'Behold, I cast out demons and perform cures today and tomorrow, and the third day I shall be perfected.' ³³Nevertheless I must journey today, tomorrow, and the day following; for it cannot be that a prophet should perish outside of Jerusalem.

³⁴"O Jerusalem, Jerusalem, the one who kills the prophets and stones those who are sent to her! How often I wanted to gather your children together, as a hen gathers her brood under her wings, but you were not willing! ³⁵See! Your house

is left to you desolate; and assuredly, I say to you, you shall not see Me until the time comes when you say, 'Blessed is He who comes in the name of the LORD!'"

109. *The Savior Teaches at a Banquet*

Lk 14:1-24 [1]Now it happened, as He went into the house of one of the rulers of the Pharisees to eat bread on the Sabbath, that they watched Him closely. [2]And behold, there was a certain man before Him who had dropsy. [3]And Jesus, answering, spoke to the lawyers and Pharisees, saying, "Is it lawful to heal on the Sabbath?"

[4]But they kept silent. And He took him and healed him, and let him go. [5]Then He answered them, saying, "Which of you, having a donkey or an ox that has fallen into a pit, will not immediately pull him out on the Sabbath day?" [6]And they could not answer Him regarding these things.

[7]So He told a parable to those who were invited, when He noted how they chose the best places, saying to them: [8]"When you are invited by anyone to a wedding feast, do not sit down in the best place, lest one more honorable than you be invited by him; [9]and he who invited you and him come and say to you, 'Give place to this man,' and then you begin with shame to take the lowest place. [10]But when you are invited, go and sit down in the lowest place, so that when he who invited you comes he may say to you, 'Friend, go up higher.' Then you will have glory in the presence of

those who sit at the table with you. ¹¹For whoever exalts himself will be humbled, and he who humbles himself will be exalted."

¹²Then He also said to him who invited Him, "When you give a dinner or a supper, do not ask your friends, your brothers, your relatives, nor rich neighbors, lest they also invite you back, and you be repaid. ¹³But when you give a feast, invite the poor, the maimed, the lame, the blind. ¹⁴And you will be blessed, because they cannot repay you; for you shall be repaid at the resurrection of the just."

¹⁵Now when one of those who sat at the table with Him heard these things, he said to Him, "Blessed is he who shall eat bread in the kingdom of God!"

¹⁶Then He said to him, "A certain man gave a great supper and invited many, ¹⁷and sent his servant at supper time to say to those who were invited, 'Come, for all things are now ready.' ¹⁸But they all with one accord began to make excuses. The first said to him, 'I have bought a piece of ground, and I must go and see it. I ask you to have me excused.' ¹⁹And another said, 'I have bought five yoke of oxen, and I am going to test them. I ask you to have me excused.' ²⁰Still another said, 'I have married a wife, and therefore I cannot come.' ²¹So that servant came and reported these things to his master. Then the master of the house, being angry, said to his servant, 'Go out quickly into the streets and lanes of the city, and bring in here the poor and the maimed and the lame and the blind.'

²²And the servant said, 'Master, it is done as you commanded, and still there is room.' ²³Then the master said to the servant, 'Go out into the highways and hedges, and compel them to come in, that my house may be filled. ²⁴For I say to you that none of those men who were invited shall taste my supper.'"

110. The Price for Following Jesus

Lk 14:25-35 ²⁵Now great multitudes went with Him. And He turned and said to them, ²⁶"If anyone comes to Me and does not hate his father and mother, wife and children, brothers and sisters, yes, and his own life also, he cannot be My disciple. ²⁷And whoever does not bear his cross and come after Me cannot be My disciple. ²⁸For which of you, intending to build a tower, does not sit down first and count the cost, whether he has enough to finish it— ²⁹lest, after he has laid the foundation, and is not able to finish, all who see it begin to mock him, ³⁰saying, 'This man began to build and was not able to finish.' ³¹Or what king, going to make war against another king, does not sit down first and consider whether he is able with ten thousand to meet him who comes against him with twenty thousand? ³²Or else, while the other is still a great way off, he sends a delegation and asks conditions of peace. ³³So likewise, whoever of you does not forsake all that he has cannot be My disciple.

³⁴"Salt is good; but if the salt has lost its flavor,

how shall it be seasoned? [35]It is neither fit for the land nor for the dunghill, but men throw it out. He who has ears to hear, let him hear!"

111. How the Lost Are Found

Lk 15:1-32 [1]Then all the tax collectors and the sinners drew near to Him to hear Him. [2]And the Pharisees and scribes complained, saying, "This Man receives sinners and eats with them." [3]So He spoke this parable to them, saying:

[4]"What man of you, having a hundred sheep, if he loses one of them, does not leave the ninety-nine in the wilderness, and go after the one which is lost until he finds it? [5]And when he has found it, he lays it on his shoulders, rejoicing. [6]And when he comes home, he calls together his friends and neighbors, saying to them, 'Rejoice with me, for I have found my sheep which was lost!' [7]I say to you that likewise there will be more joy in heaven over one sinner who repents than over ninety-nine just persons who need no repentance.

[8]"Or what woman, having ten silver coins, if she loses one coin, does not light a lamp, sweep the house, and search carefully until she finds it? [9]And when she has found it, she calls her friends and neighbors together, saying, 'Rejoice with me, for I have found the piece which I lost!' [10]Likewise, I say to you, there is joy in the presence of the angels of God over one sinner who repents."

[11]Then He said: "A certain man had two sons. [12]And the younger of them said to his father,

'Father, give me the portion of goods that falls to me.' So he divided to them his livelihood. ¹³And not many days after, the younger son gathered all together, journeyed to a far country, and there wasted his possessions with prodigal living. ¹⁴But when he had spent all, there arose a severe famine in that land, and he began to be in want. ¹⁵Then he went and joined himself to a citizen of that country, and he sent him into his fields to feed swine. ¹⁶And he would gladly have filled his stomach with the pods that the swine ate, and no one gave him anything.

¹⁷"But when he came to himself, he said, 'How many of my father's hired servants have bread enough and to spare, and I perish with hunger! ¹⁸I will arise and go to my father, and will say to him, "Father, I have sinned against heaven and before you, ¹⁹and I am no longer worthy to be called your son. Make me like one of your hired servants."'

²⁰"And he arose and came to his father. But when he was still a great way off, his father saw him and had compassion, and ran and fell on his neck and kissed him. ²¹And the son said to him, 'Father, I have sinned against heaven and in your sight, and am no longer worthy to be called your son.'

²²"But the father said to his servants, 'Bring out the best robe and put it on him, and put a ring on his hand and sandals on his feet. ²³And bring the fatted calf here and kill it, and let us eat and be merry; ²⁴for this my son was dead and is alive

again; he was lost and is found.' And they began to be merry.

²⁵"Now his older son was in the field. And as he came and drew near to the house, he heard music and dancing. ²⁶So he called one of the servants and asked what these things meant. ²⁷And he said to him, 'Your brother has come, and because he has received him safe and sound, your father has killed the fatted calf.'

²⁸"But he was angry and would not go in. Therefore his father came out and pleaded with him. ²⁹So he answered and said to his father, 'Lo, these many years I have been serving you; I never transgressed your commandment at any time; and yet you never gave me a young goat, that I might make merry with my friends. ³⁰But as soon as this son of yours came, who has devoured your livelihood with harlots, you killed the fatted calf for him.'

³¹"And he said to him, 'Son, you are always with me, and all that I have is yours. ³²It was right that we should make merry and be glad, for your brother was dead and is alive again, and was lost and is found.'"

112. Jesus Justifies Shrewdness

Lk 16:1-15 ¹He also said to His disciples: "There was a certain rich man who had a steward, and an accusation was brought to him that this man was wasting his goods. ²So he called him and said to him, 'What is this I hear about you? Give an account of your stewardship, for you can no longer be steward.'

³"Then the steward said within himself, 'What shall I do? For my master is taking the stewardship away from me. I cannot dig; I am ashamed to beg. ⁴I have resolved what to do, that when I am put out of the stewardship, they may receive me into their houses.'

⁵"So he called every one of his master's debtors to him, and said to the first, 'How much do you owe my master?' ⁶And he said, 'A hundred measures of oil.' So he said to him, 'Take your bill, and sit down quickly and write fifty.' ⁷Then he said to another, 'And how much do you owe?' So he said, 'A hundred measures of wheat.' And he said to him, 'Take your bill, and write eighty.' ⁸So the master commended the unjust steward because he had dealt shrewdly. For the sons of this world are more shrewd in their generation than the sons of light.

⁹"And I say to you, make friends for yourselves by unrighteous mammon, that when you fail, they may receive you into an everlasting home. ¹⁰He who is faithful in what is least is faithful also in much; and he who is unjust in what is least is unjust also in much. ¹¹Therefore if you have not been faithful in the unrighteous mammon, who will commit to your trust the true riches? ¹²And if you have not been faithful in what is another man's, who will give you what is your own?

¹³"No servant can serve two masters; for either

he will hate the one and love the other, or else he will be loyal to the one and despise the other. You cannot serve God and mammon."

¹⁴Now the Pharisees, who were lovers of money, also heard all these things, and they derided Him. ¹⁵And He said to them, "You are those who justify yourselves before men, but God knows your hearts. For what is highly esteemed among men is an abomination in the sight of God."

113. God's Law Holds Fast

Lk 16:16–18 ¹⁶"The law and the prophets were until John. Since that time the kingdom of God has been preached, and everyone is pressing into it. ¹⁷And it is easier for heaven and earth to pass away than for one tittle of the law to fail.

¹⁸"Whoever divorces his wife and marries another commits adultery; and whoever marries her who is divorced from her husband commits adultery."

114. A Poor Man Enters Heaven

Lk 16:19–31 ¹⁹"There was a certain rich man who was clothed in purple and fine linen and fared sumptuously every day. ²⁰But there was a certain beggar named Lazarus, full of sores, who was laid at his gate, ²¹desiring to be fed with the crumbs which fell from the rich man's table. Moreover the dogs came and licked his sores. ²²So it was that the beggar died, and was carried by the angels to Abraham's bosom. The rich man also died and was buried. [23]And being in torments in Hades, he lifted up his eyes and saw Abraham afar off, and Lazarus in his bosom.

[24]"Then he cried and said, 'Father Abraham, have mercy on me, and send Lazarus that he may dip the tip of his finger in water and cool my tongue; for I am tormented in this flame.' [25]But Abraham said, 'Son, remember that in your lifetime you received your good things, and likewise Lazarus evil things; but now he is comforted and you are tormented. [26]And besides all this, between us and you there is a great gulf fixed, so that those who want to pass from here to you cannot, nor can those from there pass to us.'

[27]"Then he said, 'I beg you therefore, father, that you would send him to my father's house, [28]for I have five brothers, that he may testify to them, lest they also come to this place of torment.' [29]Abraham said to him, 'They have Moses and the prophets; let them hear them.' [30]And he said, 'No, father Abraham; but if one goes to them from the dead, they will repent.' [31]But he said to him, 'If they do not hear Moses and the prophets, neither will they be persuaded though one rise from the dead.'"

115. Forgiveness and Faith Intertwine

Lk 17:1-10 [1]Then He said to the disciples, "It is impossible that no offenses should come, but woe to him through whom they do come! [2]It would be better for him if a millstone were hung around his neck, and he were thrown into the sea, than that he should offend one of these little ones. [3]Take heed to yourselves. If your brother sins against you, rebuke him; and if he repents, forgive him. [4]And if he sins against you seven times in a day, and seven times in a day returns to you, saying, 'I repent,' you shall forgive him."

[5]And the apostles said to the Lord, "Increase our faith."

[6]So the Lord said, "If you have faith as a mustard seed, you can say to this mulberry tree, 'Be pulled up by the roots and be planted in the sea,' and it would obey you. [7]And which of you, having a servant plowing or tending sheep, will say to him when he has come in from the field, 'Come at once and sit down to eat'? [8]But will he not rather say to him, 'Prepare something for my supper, and gird yourself and serve me till I have eaten and drunk, and afterward you will eat and drink'? [9]Does he thank that servant because he did the things that were commanded him? I think not. [10]So likewise you, when you have done all those things which you are commanded, say, 'We are unprofitable servants. We have done what was our duty to do.'"

JESUS EXPANDS
HIS MINISTRY

116. *When Jesus Meets Death*

Jn 11:1–44 ¹Now a certain man was sick, Lazarus of Bethany, the town of Mary and her sister Martha. ²It was that Mary who anointed the Lord with fragrant oil and wiped His feet with her hair, whose brother Lazarus was sick. ³Therefore the sisters sent to Him, saying, "Lord, behold, he whom You love is sick."

⁴When Jesus heard that, He said, "This sickness is not unto death, but for the glory of God, that the Son of God may be glorified through it."

⁵Now Jesus loved Martha and her sister and Lazarus. ⁶So, when He heard that he was sick, He stayed two more days in the place where He was. ⁷Then after this He said to the disciples, "Let us go to Judea again."

⁸The disciples said to Him, "Rabbi, lately the

Jews sought to stone You, and are You going there again?"

⁹Jesus answered, "Are there not twelve hours in the day? If anyone walks in the day, he does not stumble, because he sees the light of this world. ¹⁰But if one walks in the night, he stumbles, because the light is not in him." ¹¹These things He said, and after that He said to them, "Our friend Lazarus sleeps, but I go that I may wake him up."

¹²Then His disciples said, "Lord, if he sleeps he will get well." ¹³However, Jesus spoke of his death, but they thought that He was speaking about taking rest in sleep.

¹⁴Then Jesus said to them plainly, "Lazarus is dead. ¹⁵And I am glad for your sakes that I was not there, that you may believe. Nevertheless let us go to him."

¹⁶Then Thomas, who is called the Twin, said to his fellow disciples, "Let us also go, that we may die with Him."

¹⁷So when Jesus came, He found that he had already been in the tomb four days. ¹⁸Now Bethany was near Jerusalem, about two miles away. ¹⁹And many of the Jews had joined the women around Martha and Mary, to comfort them concerning their brother.

²⁰Now Martha, as soon as she heard that Jesus was coming, went and met Him, but Mary was sitting in the house. ²¹Now Martha said to Jesus, "Lord, if You had been here, my brother would not

have died. ²²But even now I know that whatever You ask of God, God will give You."

²³Jesus said to her, "Your brother will rise again."

²⁴Martha said to Him, "I know that he will rise again in the resurrection at the last day."

²⁵Jesus said to her, "I am the resurrection and the life. He who believes in Me, though he may die, he shall live. ²⁶And whoever lives and believes in Me shall never die. Do you believe this?"

²⁷She said to Him, "Yes, Lord, I believe that You are the Christ, the Son of God, who is to come into the world."

²⁸And when she had said these things, she went her way and secretly called Mary her sister, saying, "The Teacher has come and is calling for you." ²⁹As soon as she heard that, she arose quickly and came to Him. ³⁰Now Jesus had not yet come into the town, but was in the place where Martha met Him. ³¹Then the Jews who were with her in the house, and comforting her, when they saw that Mary rose up quickly and went out, followed her, saying, "She is going to the tomb to weep there."

³²Then, when Mary came where Jesus was, and saw Him, she fell down at His feet, saying to Him, "Lord, if You had been here, my brother would not have died."

³³Therefore, when Jesus saw her weeping, and the Jews who came with her weeping, He groaned in the spirit and was troubled. ³⁴And He said, "Where have you laid him?"

They said to Him, "Lord, come and see."

[35]Jesus wept. [36]Then the Jews said, "See how He loved him!"

[37]And some of them said, "Could not this Man, who opened the eyes of the blind, also have kept this man from dying?"

[38]Then Jesus, again groaning in Himself, came to the tomb. It was a cave, and a stone lay against it. [39]Jesus said, "Take away the stone."

Martha, the sister of him who was dead, said to Him, "Lord, by this time there is a stench, for he has been dead four days."

[40]Jesus said to her, "Did I not say to you that if you would believe you would see the glory of God?" [41]Then they took away the stone from the place where the dead man was lying. And Jesus lifted up His eyes and said, "Father, I thank You that You have heard Me. [42]And I know that You always hear Me, but because of the people who are standing by I said this, that they may believe that You sent Me." [43]Now when He had said these things, He cried with a loud voice, "Lazarus, come forth!" [44]And he who had died came out bound hand and foot with graveclothes, and his face was wrapped with a cloth. Jesus said to them, "Loose him, and let him go."

117. Some Disapprove of a Dead Man Raised

Jn 11:45–54 [45]Then many of the Jews who had come to Mary, and had seen the things Jesus did, believed in Him. ⁴⁶But some of them went away to the Pharisees and told them the things Jesus did. ⁴⁷Then the chief priests and the Pharisees gathered a council and said, "What shall we do? For this Man works many signs. ⁴⁸If we let Him alone like this, everyone will believe in Him, and the Romans will come and take away both our place and nation."

⁴⁹And one of them, Caiaphas, being high priest that year, said to them, "You know nothing at all, ⁵⁰nor do you consider that it is expedient for us that one man should die for the people, and not that the whole nation should perish." ⁵¹Now this he did not say on his own authority; but being high priest that year he prophesied that Jesus would die for the nation, ⁵²and not for that nation only, but also that He would gather together in one the children of God who were scattered abroad.

⁵³Then, from that day on, they plotted to put Him to death. ⁵⁴Therefore Jesus no longer walked openly among the Jews, but went from there into the country near the wilderness, to a city called Ephraim, and there remained with His disciples.

118. Thanks from One of Ten Lepers

Lk 17:11–19 ¹¹Now it happened as He went to Jerusalem that He passed through the midst of Samaria and Galilee. ¹²Then as He entered a certain village, there met Him ten men who were lepers, who stood afar off. ¹³And they lifted up their voices and said, "Jesus, Master, have mercy on us!"

¹⁴So when He saw them, He said to them,

"Go, show yourselves to the priests." And so it was that as they went, they were cleansed.

¹⁵And one of them, when he saw that he was healed, returned, and with a loud voice glorified God, ¹⁶and fell down on his face at His feet, giving Him thanks. And he was a Samaritan.

¹⁷So Jesus answered and said, "Were there not ten cleansed? But where are the nine? ¹⁸Were there not any found who returned to give glory to God except this foreigner?" ¹⁹And He said to him, "Arise, go your way. Your faith has made you well."

119. The Future Kingdom: What to Expect

Lk 17:20–37 ²⁰Now when He was asked by the Pharisees when the kingdom of God would come, He answered them and said, "The kingdom of God does not come with observation; ²¹nor will they say, 'See here!' or 'See there!' For indeed, the kingdom of God is within you."

²²Then He said to the disciples, "The days will come when you will desire to see one of the days of the Son of Man, and you will not see it. ²³And they will say to you, 'Look here!' or 'Look there!' Do not go after them or follow them. ²⁴For as the lightning that flashes out of one part under heaven shines to the other part under heaven, so also the Son of Man will be in His day. ²⁵But first He must suffer many things and be rejected by this generation. ²⁶And as it was in the days of Noah, so it will

bo alco in tho days of tho Son of Man. ²⁷They ate, they drank, they married wives, they were given in marriage, until the day that Noah entered the ark, and the flood came and destroyed them all. ²⁸Likewise as it was also in the days of Lot: They ate, they drank, they bought, they sold, they planted, they built; ²⁹but on the day that Lot went out of Sodom it rained fire and brimstone from heaven and destroyed them all. ³⁰Even so will it be in the day when the Son of Man is revealed.

³¹"In that day, he who is on the housetop, and his goods are in the house, let him not come down to take them away. And likewise the one who is in the field, let him not turn back. ³²Remember Lot's wife. ³³Whoever seeks to save his life will lose it, and whoever loses his life will preserve it. ³⁴I tell you, in that night there will be two men in one bed: the one will be taken and the other will be left. ³⁵Two women will be grinding together: the one will be taken and the other left. ³⁶Two men will be in the field: the one will be taken and the other left."

³⁷And they answered and said to Him, "Where, Lord?"

So He said to them, "Wherever the body is, there the eagles will be gathered together."

120. Prayer Provides Interesting Tales

Lk 18:1-14 ¹Then He spoke a parable to them, that men always ought to pray and not lose heart, ²saying: "There was in a certain city a judge who did not fear God nor regard man. ³Now there was a widow in that city; and she came to him, saying, 'Get justice for me from my adversary.' ⁴And he would not for a while; but afterward he said within himself, 'Though I do not fear God nor regard man, ⁵yet because this widow troubles me I will avenge her, lest by her continual coming she weary me.'"

⁶Then the Lord said, "Hear what the unjust judge said. ⁷And shall God not avenge His own elect who cry out day and night to Him, though He bears long with them? ⁸I tell you that He will avenge them speedily. Nevertheless, when the Son of Man comes, will He really find faith on the earth?"

⁹Also He spoke this parable to some who trusted in themselves that they were righteous, and despised others: ¹⁰"Two men went up to the temple to pray, one a Pharisee and the other a tax collector. ¹¹The Pharisee stood and prayed thus with himself, 'God, I thank You that I am not like other men—extortioners, unjust, adulterers, or even as this tax collector. ¹²I fast twice a week; I give tithes of all that I possess.' ¹³And the tax collector, standing afar off, would not so much as raise his eyes to heaven, but beat his breast, saying, 'God, be merciful to me a sinner!' ¹⁴I tell you, this man went down to his house justified rather than the other; for everyone who exalts himself will be humbled, and he who humbles himself will be exalted."

A SHORT RETURN VISIT
TO PEREA

121. Teaching, Ever Teaching

Mk 10:1–2 ¹Then He arose from there and came to the region of Judea by the other side of the Jordan. And multitudes gathered to Him again, and as He was accustomed, He taught them again.

²The Pharisees came and asked Him, "Is it lawful for a man to divorce his wife?" testing Him.

122. Jesus Discusses Divorce

Matt 19:3–12 ³The Pharisees also came to Him, testing Him, and saying to Him, "Is it lawful for a man to divorce his wife for just any reason?"

⁴And He answered and said to them, "Have you not read that He who made them at the beginning 'made them male and female,' ⁵and said, 'For this reason a man shall leave his father and mother

and be joined to his wife, and the two shall become one flesh'? ⁶So then, they are no longer two but one flesh. Therefore what God has joined together, let not man separate."

⁷They said to Him, "Why then did Moses command to give a certificate of divorce, and to put her away?"

⁸He said to them, "Moses, because of the hardness of your hearts, permitted you to divorce your wives, but from the beginning it was not so. ⁹And I say to you, whoever divorces his wife, except for sexual immorality, and marries another, commits adultery; and whoever marries her who is divorced commits adultery."

¹⁰His disciples said to Him, "If such is the case of the man with his wife, it is better not to marry."

¹¹But He said to them, "All cannot accept this saying, but only those to whom it has been given: ¹²For there are eunuchs who were born thus from their mother's womb, and there are eunuchs who were made eunuchs by men, and there are eunuchs who have made themselves eunuchs for the kingdom of heaven's sake. He who is able to accept it, let him accept it."

Mk 10:10–12 ¹⁰In the house His disciples also asked Him again about the same matter. ¹¹So He said to them, "Whoever divorces his wife and marries another commits adultery against her. ¹²And if a woman divorces her husband and marries another, she commits adultery."

Mk 10:13–16 ¹³Then they brought little children to Him, that He might touch them; but the disciples rebuked those who brought them. ¹⁴But when Jesus saw it, He was greatly displeased and said to them, "Let the little children come to Me, and do not forbid them; for of such is the kingdom of God. ¹⁵Assuredly, I say to you, whoever does not receive the kingdom of God as a little child will by no means enter it." ¹⁶And He took them up in His arms, laid His hands on them, and blessed them.

124. On Things Important

Mk 10:17–31 ¹⁷Now as He was going out on the road, one came running, knelt before Him, and asked Him, "Good Teacher, what shall I do that I may inherit eternal life?"

¹⁸So Jesus said to him, "Why do you call Me good? No one is good but One, that is, God. ¹⁹You know the commandments: 'Do not commit adultery,' 'Do not murder,' 'Do not steal,' 'Do not bear false witness,' 'Do not defraud,' 'Honor your father and your mother.'"

²⁰And he answered and said to Him, "Teacher, all these things I have kept from my youth."

²¹Then Jesus, looking at him, loved him, and said to him, "One thing you lack: Go your way, sell whatever you have and give to the poor, and you

will have treasure in heaven; and come, take up the cross, and follow Me."

²²But he was sad at this word, and went away sorrowful, for he had great possessions.

²³Then Jesus looked around and said to His disciples, "How hard it is for those who have riches to enter the kingdom of God!" ²⁴And the disciples were astonished at His words. But Jesus answered again and said to them, "Children, how hard it is for those who trust in riches to enter the kingdom of God! ²⁵It is easier for a camel to go through the eye of a needle than for a rich man to enter the kingdom of God."

²⁶And they were greatly astonished, saying among themselves, "Who then can be saved?"

²⁷But Jesus looked at them and said, "With men it is impossible, but not with God; for with God all things are possible."

²⁸Then Peter began to say to Him, "See, we have left all and followed You."

²⁹So Jesus answered and said, "Assuredly, I say to you, there is no one who has left house or brothers or sisters or father or mother or wife or children or lands, for My sake and the gospel's, ³⁰who shall not receive a hundredfold now in this time—houses and brothers and sisters and mothers and children and lands, with persecutions—and in the age to come, eternal life. ³¹But many who are first will be last, and the last first."

Matt 20:1-16 [1]"For the kingdom of heaven is like a landowner who went out early in the morning to hire laborers for his vineyard. [2]Now when he had agreed with the laborers for a denarius a day, he sent them into his vineyard. [3]And he went out about the third hour and saw others standing idle in the marketplace, [4]and said to them, 'You also go into the vineyard, and whatever is right I will give you.' So they went. [5]Again he went out about the sixth and the ninth hour, and did likewise. [6]And about the eleventh hour he went out and found others standing idle, and said to them, 'Why have you been standing here idle all day?' [7]They said to him, 'Because no one hired us.' He said to them, 'You also go into the vineyard, and whatever is right you will receive.'

[8]"So when evening had come, the owner of the vineyard said to his steward, 'Call the laborers and give them their wages, beginning with the last to the first.' [9]And when those came who were hired about the eleventh hour, they each received a denarius. [10]But when the first came, they supposed that they would receive more; and they likewise received each a denarius. [11]And when they had received it, they complained against the landowner, [12]saying, 'These last men have worked only one hour, and you made them equal to us who have borne the burden and the heat of the day.' [13]But he answered one of them and said, 'Friend, I

am doing you no wrong. Did you not agree with me for a denarius? ¹⁴Take what is yours and go your way. I wish to give to this last man the same as to you. ¹⁵Is it not lawful for me to do what I wish with my own things? Or is your eye evil because I am good?' ¹⁶So the last will be first, and the first last. For many are called, but few chosen."

126. Death Is in the Picture

Mk 10:32–34 ³²Now they were on the road, going up to Jerusalem, and Jesus was going before them; and they were amazed. And as they followed they were afraid. Then He took the twelve aside again and began to tell them the things that would happen to Him: ³³"Behold, we are going up to Jerusalem, and the Son of Man will be betrayed to the chief priests and to the scribes; and they will condemn Him to death and deliver Him to the Gentiles; ³⁴and they will mock Him, and scourge Him, and spit on Him, and kill Him. And the third day He will rise again."

Lk 18:34 ³⁴But they understood none of these things; this saying was hidden from them, and they did not know the things which were spoken.

127. Selfishness Has No Place

Mk 10:35–45 ³⁵Then James and John, the sons of Zebedee, came to Him, saying, "Teacher, we want You to do for us whatever we ask."

³⁶And He said to them, "What do you want Me to do for you?"

³⁷They said to Him, "Grant us that we may sit, one on Your right hand and the other on Your left, in Your glory."

³⁸But Jesus said to them, "You do not know what you ask. Are you able to drink the cup that I drink, and be baptized with the baptism that I am baptized with?"

³⁹They said to Him, "We are able."

So Jesus said to them, "You will indeed drink the cup that I drink, and with the baptism I am baptized with you will be baptized; ⁴⁰but to sit on My right hand and on My left is not Mine to give, but it is for those for whom it is prepared."

⁴¹And when the ten heard it, they began to be greatly displeased with James and John. ⁴²But Jesus called them to Himself and said to them, "You know that those who are considered rulers over the Gentiles lord it over them, and their great ones exercise authority over them. ⁴³Yet it shall not be so among you; but whoever desires to become great among you shall be your servant. ⁴⁴And whoever of you desires to be first shall be slave of all. ⁴⁵For even the Son of Man did not come to be served, but to serve, and to give His life a ransom for many."

JESUS RETURNS
AMIDST HOSTILITY

128. Jesus Among the Blind

Mk 10:46–52 ⁴⁶Now they came to Jericho. As He
went out of Jericho with His disciples and a great
multitude, blind Bartimaeus, the son of Timaeus,
sat by the road begging. ⁴⁷And when he heard that
it was Jesus of Nazareth, he began to cry out and
say, "Jesus, Son of David, have mercy on me!"

⁴⁸Then many warned him to be quiet; but he
cried out all the more, "Son of David, have mercy
on me!"

⁴⁹So Jesus stood still and commanded him to
be called.

Then they called the blind man, saying to him,
"Be of good cheer. Rise, He is calling you."

⁵⁰And throwing aside his garment, he rose and
came to Jesus.

⁵¹So Jesus answered and said to him, "What do
you want Me to do for you?"

The blind man said to Him, "Rabboni, that I may receive my sight."

⁵²Then Jesus said to him, "Go your way; your faith has made you well." And immediately he received his sight and followed Jesus on the road.

129. Collecting Taxes and Souls

Lk 19:1–10 ¹Then Jesus entered and passed through Jericho. ²Now behold, there was a man named Zacchaeus who was a chief tax collector, and he was rich. ³And he sought to see who Jesus was, but could not because of the crowd, for he was of short stature. ⁴So he ran ahead and climbed up into a sycamore tree to see Him, for He was going to pass that way. ⁵And when Jesus came to the place, He looked up and saw him, and said to him, "Zacchaeus, make haste and come down, for today I must stay at your house." ⁶So he made haste and came down, and received Him joyfully. ⁷But when they saw it, they all complained, saying, "He has gone to be a guest with a man who is a sinner."

⁸Then Zacchaeus stood and said to the Lord, "Look, Lord, I give half of my goods to the poor; and if I have taken anything from anyone by false accusation, I restore fourfold."

⁹And Jesus said to him, "Today salvation has come to this house, because he also is a son of Abraham; ¹⁰for the Son of Man has come to seek and to save that which was lost."

130. Working Your Talents—Not Your Tongue

Lk 19:11-28 ¹¹Now as they heard these things, He spoke another parable, because He was near Jerusalem and because they thought the kingdom of God would appear immediately. ¹²Therefore He said: "A certain nobleman went into a far country to receive for himself a kingdom and to return. ¹³So he called ten of his servants, delivered to them ten minas, and said to them, 'Do business till I come.' ¹⁴But his citizens hated him, and sent a delegation after him, saying, 'We will not have this man to reign over us.'

¹⁵"And so it was that when he returned, having received the kingdom, he then commanded these servants, to whom he had given the money, to be called to him, that he might know how much every man had gained by trading. ¹⁶Then came the first, saying, 'Master, your mina has earned ten minas.' ¹⁷And he said to him, 'Well done, good servant; because you were faithful in a very little, have authority over ten cities.' ¹⁸And the second came, saying, 'Master, your mina has earned five minas.' ¹⁹Likewise he said to him, 'You also be over five cities.'

²⁰"Then another came, saying, 'Master, here is your mina, which I have kept put away in a handkerchief. ²¹For I feared you, because you are an austere man. You collect what you did not deposit, and reap what you did not sow.' ²²And he said to

him, 'Out of your own mouth I will judge you, you wicked servant. You knew that I was an austere man, collecting what I did not deposit and reaping what I did not sow. ²³Why then did you not put my money in the bank, that at my coming I might have collected it with interest?'

²⁴"And he said to those who stood by, 'Take the mina from him, and give it to him who has ten minas.' ²⁵(But they said to him, 'Master, he has ten minas.') ²⁶'For I say to you, that to everyone who has will be given; and from him who does not have, even what he has will be taken away from him. ²⁷But bring here those enemies of mine, who did not want me to reign over them, and slay them before me.'"

²⁸When He had said this, He went on ahead, going up to Jerusalem.

131. He Walked Amid Hostility

Jn 11:55-57 ⁵⁵And the Passover of the Jews was near, and many went from the country up to Jerusalem before the Passover, to purify themselves. ⁵⁶Then they sought Jesus, and spoke among themselves as they stood in the temple, "What do you think—that He will not come to the feast?" ⁵⁷Now both the chief priests and the Pharisees had given a command, that if anyone knew where He was, he should report it, that they might seize Him.

Jn 12:1 ¹Then, six days before the Passover, Jesus came to Bethany, where Lazarus was who had been dead, whom He had raised from the dead.

Jn 12:9-11 ⁹Now a great many of the Jews knew that He was there; and they came, not for Jesus' sake only, but that they might also see Lazarus, whom He had raised from the dead. ¹⁰But the chief priests plotted to put Lazarus to death also, ¹¹because on account of him many of the Jews went away and believed in Jesus.

LAST EFFORTS IN JERUSALEM

132. Fit Welcome for a King

Mk 11:1–10 ¹Now when they drew near Jerusalem, to Bethphage and Bethany, at the Mount of Olives, He sent two of His disciples; ²and He said to them, "Go into the village opposite you; and as soon as you have entered it you will find a colt tied, on which no one has sat. Loose it and bring it. ³And if anyone says to you, 'Why are you doing this?' say, 'The Lord has need of it,' and immediately he will send it here."

⁴So they went their way, and found the colt tied by the door outside on the street, and they loosed it. ⁵But some of those who stood there said to them, "What are you doing, loosing the colt?"

⁶And they spoke to them just as Jesus had commanded. So they let them go. ⁷Then they brought the colt to Jesus and threw their clothes on it, and He sat on it. ⁸And many spread their clothes on the road, and others cut down leafy branches from the trees and spread them on the road. ⁹Then

those who went before and those who followed cried out, saying:

> "Hosanna!
> 'Blessed is He who comes in the name of
>   the LORD!'
> 10 Blessed is the kingdom of our father David
>   That comes in the name of the Lord!
>   Hosanna in the highest!"

Jn 12:17–19 ¹⁷Therefore the people, who were with Him when He called Lazarus out of his tomb and raised him from the dead, bore witness. ¹⁸For this reason the people also met Him, because they heard that He had done this sign. ¹⁹The Pharisees therefore said among themselves, "You see that you are accomplishing nothing. Look, the world has gone after Him!"

Lk 19:39–40 ³⁹And some of the Pharisees called to Him from the crowd, "Teacher, rebuke Your disciples."

⁴⁰But He answered and said to them, "I tell you that if these should keep silent, the stones would immediately cry out."

Matt 21:4–5 ⁴All this was done that it might be fulfilled which was spoken by the prophet, saying:

> ⁵ "Tell the daughter of Zion,
>   'Behold, your King is coming to you,
>   Lowly, and sitting on a donkey,
>   A colt, the foal of a donkey.'"

Jn 12:16 [16]His disciples did not understand these things at first; but when Jesus was glorified, then they remembered that these things were written about Him and that they had done these things to Him.

Lk 19:41–44 [41]Now as He drew near, He saw the city and wept over it, [42]saying, "If you had known, even you, especially in this your day, the things that make for your peace! But now they are hidden from your eyes. [43]For days will come upon you when your enemies will build an embankment around you, surround you and close you in on every side, [44]and level you, and your children within you, to the ground; and they will not leave in you one stone upon another, because you did not know the time of your visitation."

Matt 21:10–11 [10]And when He had come into Jerusalem, all the city was moved, saying, "Who is this?"

[11]So the multitudes said, "This is Jesus, the prophet from Nazareth of Galilee."

Mk 11:11 [11]And Jesus went into Jerusalem and into the temple. So when He had looked around at all things, as the hour was already late, He went out to Bethany with the twelve.

133. When No Production Means No Life

Mk 11:12–14 [12]Now the next day, when they had come out from Bethany, He was hungry. [13]And seeing from afar a fig tree having leaves, He went

to see if perhaps He would find something on it.
When He came to it, He found nothing but leaves,
for it was not the season for figs. ¹⁴In response
Jesus said to it, "Let no one eat fruit from you ever
again."

And His disciples heard it.

134. More Temple Cleaning by Jesus

Mk 11:15–18 ¹⁵So they came to Jerusalem. Then
Jesus went into the temple and began to drive out
those who bought and sold in the temple, and
overturned the tables of the money changers and
the seats of those who sold doves. ¹⁶And He would
not allow anyone to carry wares through the temple. ¹⁷Then He taught, saying to them, "Is it not
written, 'My house shall be called a house of prayer
for all nations'? But you have made it a 'den of
thieves.'"

¹⁸And the scribes and chief priests heard it and
sought how they might destroy Him; for they
feared Him, because all the people were astonished
at His teaching.

Matt 21:14–16 ¹⁴Then the blind and the lame came
to Him in the temple, and He healed them. ¹⁵But
when the chief priests and scribes saw the wonderful things that He did, and the children crying out in
the temple and saying, "Hosanna to the Son of
David!" they were indignant ¹⁶and said to Him, "Do
You hear what these are saying?"

And Jesus said to them, "Yes. Have you never
read,

'Out of the mouth of babes and nursing
infants
You have perfected praise'?"

135. Greek Curiosity and a Sermon on Death

Jn 12:20-50 ²⁰Now there were certain Greeks among those who came up to worship at the feast. ²¹Then they came to Philip, who was from Bethsaida of Galilee, and asked him, saying, "Sir, we wish to see Jesus."

²²Philip came and told Andrew, and in turn Andrew and Philip told Jesus.

²³But Jesus answered them, saying, "The hour has come that the Son of Man should be glorified. ²⁴Most assuredly, I say to you, unless a grain of wheat falls into the ground and dies, it remains alone; but if it dies, it produces much grain. ²⁵He who loves his life will lose it, and he who hates his life in this world will keep it for eternal life. ²⁶If anyone serves Me, let him follow Me; and where I am, there My servant will be also. If anyone serves Me, him My Father will honor.

²⁷"Now My soul is troubled, and what shall I say? 'Father, save Me from this hour'? But for this purpose I came to this hour. ²⁸Father, glorify Your name."

Then a voice came from heaven, saying, "I have both glorified it and will glorify it again."

²⁹Therefore the people who stood by and

heard it said that it had thundered. Others said, "An angel has spoken to Him."

³⁰Jesus answered and said, "This voice did not come because of Me, but for your sake. ³¹Now is the judgment of this world; now the ruler of this world will be cast out. ³²And I, if I am lifted up from the earth, will draw all peoples to Myself." ³³This He said, signifying by what death He would die.

³⁴The people answered Him, "We have heard from the law that the Christ remains forever; and how can You say, 'The Son of Man must be lifted up'? Who is this Son of Man?"

³⁵Then Jesus said to them, "A little while longer the light is with you. Walk while you have the light, lest darkness overtake you; he who walks in darkness does not know where he is going. ³⁶While you have the light, believe in the light, that you may become sons of light." These things Jesus spoke, and departed, and was hidden from them.

³⁷But although He had done so many signs before them, they did not believe in Him, ³⁸that the word of Isaiah the prophet might be fulfilled, which he spoke:

"Lord, who has believed our report?
And to whom has the arm of the LORD
been revealed?"

³⁹Therefore they could not believe, because Isaiah said again:

⁴⁰ "He has blinded their eyes and hardened
   their hearts,
   Lest they should see with their eyes,
   Lest they should understand with their
      hearts and turn,
   So that I should heal them."

⁴¹These things Isaiah said when he saw His glory and spoke of Him.

⁴²Nevertheless even among the rulers many believed in Him, but because of the Pharisees they did not confess Him, lest they should be put out of the synagogue; ⁴³for they loved the praise of men more than the praise of God.

⁴⁴Then Jesus cried out and said, "He who believes in Me, believes not in Me but in Him who sent Me. ⁴⁵And he who sees Me sees Him who sent Me. ⁴⁶I have come as a light into the world, that whoever believes in Me should not abide in darkness. ⁴⁷And if anyone hears My words and does not believe, I do not judge him; for I did not come to judge the world but to save the world. ⁴⁸He who rejects Me, and does not receive My words, has that which judges him—the word that I have spoken will judge him in the last day. ⁴⁹For I have not spoken on My own authority; but the Father who sent Me gave Me a command, what I should say and what I should speak. ⁵⁰And I know that His command is everlasting life. Therefore, whatever I speak, just as the Father has told Me, so I speak."

Matt 21:17 ¹⁷Then He left them and went out of the city to Bethany, and He lodged there.

136. Tree Cursed by Jesus Teaches a Lesson

Mk 11:20-25 ²⁰Now in the morning, as they passed by, they saw the fig tree dried up from the roots. ²¹And Peter, remembering, said to Him, "Rabbi, look! The fig tree which You cursed has withered away."

²²So Jesus answered and said to them, "Have faith in God. ²³For assuredly, I say to you, whoever says to this mountain, 'Be removed and be cast into the sea,' and does not doubt in his heart, but believes that those things he says will be done, he will have whatever he says. ²⁴Therefore I say to you, whatever things you ask when you pray, believe that you receive them, and you will have them.

²⁵"And whenever you stand praying, if you have anything against anyone, forgive him, that your Father in heaven may also forgive you your trespasses."

137. Earthly Stories Answer Questions

Matt 12:23-46 ²³And all the multitudes were amazed and said, "Could this be the Son of David?"

²⁴Now when the Pharisees heard it they said, "This fellow does not cast out demons except by Beelzebub, the ruler of the demons."

²⁵But Jesus knew their thoughts, and said to them: "Every kingdom divided against itself is brought to desolation, and every city or house divided against itself will not stand. ²⁶If Satan casts out Satan, he is divided against himself. How then will his kingdom stand? ²⁷And if I cast out demons by Beelzebub, by whom do your sons cast them out? Therefore they shall be your judges. ²⁸But if I cast out demons by the Spirit of God, surely the kingdom of God has come upon you. ²⁹Or how can one enter a strong man's house and plunder his goods, unless he first binds the strong man? And then he will plunder his house. ³⁰He who is not with Me is against Me, and he who does not gather with Me scatters abroad.

³¹"Therefore I say to you, every sin and blasphemy will be forgiven men, but the blasphemy against the Spirit will not be forgiven men. ³²Anyone who speaks a word against the Son of Man, it will be forgiven him; but whoever speaks against the Holy Spirit, it will not be forgiven him, either in this age or in the age to come.

³³"Either make the tree good and its fruit good, or else make the tree bad and its fruit bad; for a tree is known by its fruit. ³⁴Brood of vipers! How can you, being evil, speak good things? For out of the abundance of the heart the mouth speaks. ³⁵A good man out of the good treasure of his heart brings forth good things, and an evil man out of the evil treasure brings forth evil things. ³⁶But I say to you that for every idle word men may speak, they

will give account of it in the day of judgment. ³⁷For by your words you will be justified, and by your words you will be condemned."

³⁸Then some of the scribes and Pharisees answered, saying, "Teacher, we want to see a sign from You."

³⁹But He answered and said to them, "An evil and adulterous generation seeks after a sign, and no sign will be given to it except the sign of the prophet Jonah. ⁴⁰For as Jonah was three days and three nights in the belly of the great fish, so will the Son of Man be three days and three nights in the heart of the earth. ⁴¹The men of Nineveh will rise up in the judgment with this generation and condemn it, because they repented at the preaching of Jonah; and indeed a greater than Jonah is here. ⁴²The queen of the South will rise up in the judgment with this generation and condemn it, for she came from the ends of the earth to hear the wisdom of Solomon; and indeed a greater than Solomon is here.

⁴³"When an unclean spirit goes out of a man, he goes through dry places, seeking rest, and finds none. ⁴⁴Then he says, 'I will return to my house from which I came.' And when he comes, he finds it empty, swept, and put in order. ⁴⁵Then he goes and takes with him seven other spirits more wicked than himself, and they enter and dwell there; and the last state of that man is worse than the first. So shall it also be with this wicked generation."

"While He was still talking to the multitudes, behold, His mother and brothers stood outside, seeking to speak with Him.

Lk 20:19 ¹⁹And the chief priests and the scribes that very hour sought to lay hands on Him, but they feared the people—for they knew He had spoken this parable against them.

138. Jesus Won't Be Trapped over Taxes

Mk 12:13–17 ¹³Then they sent to Him some of the Pharisees and the Herodians, to catch Him in His words. ¹⁴When they had come, they said to Him, "Teacher, we know that You are true, and care about no one; for You do not regard the person of men, but teach the way of God in truth. Is it lawful to pay taxes to Caesar, or not? ¹⁵Shall we pay, or shall we not pay?"

But He, knowing their hypocrisy, said to them, "Why do you test Me? Bring Me a denarius that I may see it." ¹⁶So they brought it.

And He said to them, "Whose image and inscription is this?" They said to Him, "Caesar's."

¹⁷And Jesus answered and said to them, "Render to Caesar the things that are Caesar's, and to God the things that are God's."

And they marveled at Him.

Lk 20:26 ²⁶But they could not catch Him in His words in the presence of the people. And they marveled at His answer and kept silent.

139. *The Sadducees Are Satisfied*

Lk 20:27-33 ²⁷Then some of the Sadducees, who deny that there is a resurrection, came to Him and asked Him, ²⁸saying: "Teacher, Moses wrote to us that if a man's brother dies, having a wife, and he dies without children, his brother should take his wife and raise up offspring for his brother. ²⁹Now there were seven brothers. And the first took a wife, and died without children. ³⁰And the second took her as wife, and he died childless. ³¹Then the third took her, and in like manner the seven also; and they left no children, and died. ³²Last of all the woman died also. ³³Therefore, in the resurrection, whose wife does she become? For all seven had her as wife."

Matt 22:29 ²⁹Jesus answered and said to them, "You are mistaken, not knowing the Scriptures nor the power of God."

Lk 20:34-40 ³⁴Jesus answered and said to them, "The sons of this age marry and are given in marriage. ³⁵But those who are counted worthy to attain that age, and the resurrection from the dead, neither marry nor are given in marriage; ³⁶nor can they die anymore, for they are equal to the angels and are sons of God, being sons of the resurrection. ³⁷But even Moses showed in the burning bush passage that the dead are raised, when he called the Lord 'the God of Abraham, the God of Isaac, and the God of Jacob.' ³⁸For He is not the God of the dead but of the living, for all live to Him."

³⁹Then some of the scribes answered and said, "Teacher, You have spoken well." ⁴⁰But after that they dared not question Him anymore.

140. Two Commandments Are Greatest

Mk 12:28-34 ²⁸Then one of the scribes came, and having heard them reasoning together, perceiving that He had answered them well, asked Him, "Which is the first commandment of all?"

²⁹Jesus answered him, "The first of all the commandments is: 'Hear, O Israel, the LORD our God, the LORD is one. ³⁰And you shall love the LORD your God with all your heart, with all your soul, with all your mind, and with all your strength.' This is the first commandment. ³¹And the second, like it, is this: 'You shall love your neighbor as yourself.' There is no other commandment greater than these."

³²So the scribe said to Him, "Well said, Teacher. You have spoken the truth, for there is one God, and there is no other but He. ³³And to love Him with all the heart, with all the understanding, with all the soul, and with all the strength, and to love one's neighbor as oneself, is more than all the whole burnt offerings and sacrifices."

³⁴Now when Jesus saw that he answered wisely, He said to him, "You are not far from the kingdom of God."

But after that no one dared question Him.

Lk 21:37 ³⁷And in the daytime He was teaching in

the temple, but at night He went out and stayed on the mountain called Olivet.

141. More from the Pharisees

Lk 21:38 ³⁸Then early in the morning all the people came to Him in the temple to hear Him.

Matt 22:41–46 ⁴¹While the Pharisees were gathered together, Jesus asked them, ⁴²saying, "What do you think about the Christ? Whose Son is He?"

They said to Him, "The Son of David."

⁴³He said to them, "How then does David in the Spirit call Him 'Lord,' saying:

⁴⁴ 'The LORD said to my Lord,
  "Sit at My right hand,
    Till I make Your enemies Your foot-
        stool"'?

⁴⁵If David then calls Him 'Lord,' how is He his Son?" ⁴⁶And no one was able to answer Him a word, nor from that day on did anyone dare question Him anymore.

142. Jesus Abhors False Teaching

Matt 23:1–7 ¹Then Jesus spoke to the multitudes and to His disciples, ²saying: "The scribes and the Pharisees sit in Moses' seat. ³Therefore whatever they tell you to observe, that observe and do, but do not do according to their works; for they say, and do not do. ⁴For they bind heavy burdens, hard to bear, and lay them on men's shoulders; but they themselves will not move them with one of their fingers. 5But all their works they do to be seen by men. They make their phylacteries broad and enlarge the borders of their garments. 6They love the best places at feasts, the best seats in the synagogues, 7greetings in the marketplaces, and to be called by men, 'Rabbi, Rabbi.'

Mk 12:40 40"[They] devour widows' houses, and for a pretense make long prayers. These will receive greater condemnation."

Matt 23:8–39 8"But you, do not be called 'Rabbi'; for One is your Teacher, the Christ, and you are all brethren. 9Do not call anyone on earth your father; for One is your Father, He who is in heaven. 10And do not be called teachers; for One is your Teacher, the Christ. 11But he who is greatest among you shall be your servant. 12And whoever exalts himself will be humbled, and he who humbles himself will be exalted.

13"But woe to you, scribes and Pharisees, hypocrites! For you shut up the kingdom of heaven against men; for you neither go in yourselves, nor do you allow those who are entering to go in. 14Woe to you, scribes and Pharisees, hypocrites! For you devour widows' houses, and for a pretense make long prayers. Therefore you will receive greater condemnation.

15"Woe to you, scribes and Pharisees, hypocrites! For you travel land and sea to win one proselyte, and when he is won, you make him twice as much a son of hell as yourselves.

¹⁶"Woe to you, blind guides, who say, 'Whoever swears by the temple, it is nothing; but whoever swears by the gold of the temple, he is obliged to perform it.' ¹⁷Fools and blind! For which is greater, the gold or the temple that sanctifies the gold? ¹⁸And, 'Whoever swears by the altar, it is nothing; but whoever swears by the gift that is on it, he is obliged to perform it.' ¹⁹Fools and blind! For which is greater, the gift or the altar that sanctifies the gift? ²⁰Therefore he who swears by the altar, swears by it and by all things on it. ²¹He who swears by the temple, swears by it and by Him who dwells in it. ²²And he who swears by heaven, swears by the throne of God and by Him who sits on it.

²³"Woe to you, scribes and Pharisees, hypocrites! For you pay tithe of mint and anise and cummin, and have neglected the weightier matters of the law: justice and mercy and faith. These you ought to have done, without leaving the others undone. ²⁴Blind guides, who strain out a gnat and swallow a camel!

²⁵"Woe to you, scribes and Pharisees, hypocrites! For you cleanse the outside of the cup and dish, but inside they are full of extortion and self-indulgence. ²⁶Blind Pharisee, first cleanse the inside of the cup and dish, that the outside of them may be clean also.

²⁷"Woe to you, scribes and Pharisees, hypocrites! For you are like whitewashed tombs which indeed appear beautiful outwardly, but inside are

full of dead men's bones and all uncleanness. [28]Even so you also outwardly appear righteous to men, but inside you are full of hypocrisy and lawlessness.

[29]"Woe to you, scribes and Pharisees, hypocrites! Because you build the tombs of the prophets and adorn the monuments of the righteous, [30]and say, 'If we had lived in the days of our fathers, we would not have been partakers with them in the blood of the prophets.'

[31]"Therefore you are witnesses against yourselves that you are sons of those who murdered the prophets. [32]Fill up, then, the measure of your fathers' guilt. [33]Serpents, brood of vipers! How can you escape the condemnation of hell? [34]Therefore, indeed, I send you prophets, wise men, and scribes: some of them you will kill and crucify, and some of them you will scourge in your synagogues and persecute from city to city, [35]that on you may come all the righteous blood shed on the earth, from the blood of righteous Abel to the blood of Zechariah, son of Berechiah, whom you murdered between the temple and the altar. [36]Assuredly, I say to you, all these things will come upon this generation.

[37]"O Jerusalem, Jerusalem, the one who kills the prophets and stones those who are sent to her! How often I wanted to gather your children together, as a hen gathers her chicks under her wings, but you were not willing! [38]See! Your house is left to you desolate; [39]for I say to you, you shall

see Me no more till you say, 'Blessed is He who comes in the name of the LORD!'"

143. When a Little Means a Lot

Mk 12:41-44 ⁴¹Now Jesus sat opposite the treasury and saw how the people put money into the treasury. And many who were rich put in much. ⁴²Then one poor widow came and threw in two mites, which make a quadrans. ⁴³So He called His disciples to Himself and said to them, "Assuredly, I say to you that this poor widow has put in more than all those who have given to the treasury; ⁴⁴for they all put in out of their abundance, but she out of her poverty put in all that she had, her whole livelihood."

SHADOWS OF THE CROSS

144. *Jesus Talks of Dying*

Matt 24:1–50 ¹Then Jesus went out and departed from the temple, and His disciples came up to show Him the buildings of the temple. ²And Jesus said to them, "Do you not see all these things? Assuredly, I say to you, not one stone shall be left here upon another, that shall not be thrown down."

³Now as He sat on the Mount of Olives, the disciples came to Him privately, saying, "Tell us, when will these things be? And what will be the sign of Your coming, and of the end of the age?"

⁴And Jesus answered and said to them: "Take heed that no one deceives you. ⁵For many will come in My name, saying, 'I am the Christ,' and will deceive many. ⁶And you will hear of wars and rumors of wars. See that you are not troubled; for all these things must come to pass, but the end is not yet. ⁷For nation will rise against nation, and kingdom against kingdom. And there will be fam-

ines, pestilences, and earthquakes in various places. ⁸All these are the beginning of sorrows.

⁹"Then they will deliver you up to tribulation and kill you, and you will be hated by all nations for My name's sake. ¹⁰And then many will be offended, will betray one another, and will hate one another. ¹¹Then many false prophets will rise up and deceive many. ¹²And because lawlessness will abound, the love of many will grow cold. ¹³But he who endures to the end shall be saved. ¹⁴And this gospel of the kingdom will be preached in all the world as a witness to all the nations, and then the end will come.

¹⁵"Therefore when you see the 'abomination of desolation,' spoken of by Daniel the prophet, standing in the holy place" (whoever reads, let him understand), ¹⁶"then let those who are in Judea flee to the mountains. ¹⁷Let him who is on the housetop not go down to take anything out of his house. ¹⁸And let him who is in the field not go back to get his clothes. ¹⁹But woe to those who are pregnant and to those who are nursing babies in those days! ²⁰And pray that your flight may not be in winter or on the Sabbath. ²¹For then there will be great tribulation, such as has not been since the beginning of the world until this time, no, nor ever shall be. ²²And unless those days were shortened, no flesh would be saved; but for the elect's sake those days will be shortened.

²³"Then if anyone says to you, 'Look, here is the Christ!' or 'There!' do not believe it. ²⁴For false

christs and false prophets will rise and show great signs and wonders to deceive, if possible, even the elect. ²⁵See, I have told you beforehand.

²⁶"Therefore if they say to you, 'Look, He is in the desert!' do not go out; or 'Look, He is in the inner rooms!' do not believe it. ²⁷For as the lightning comes from the east and flashes to the west, so also will the coming of the Son of Man be. ²⁸For wherever the carcass is, there the eagles will be gathered together.

²⁹"Immediately after the tribulation of those days the sun will be darkened, and the moon will not give its light; the stars will fall from heaven, and the powers of the heavens will be shaken. ³⁰Then the sign of the Son of Man will appear in heaven, and then all the tribes of the earth will mourn, and they will see the Son of Man coming on the clouds of heaven with power and great glory. ³¹And He will send His angels with a great sound of a trumpet, and they will gather together His elect from the four winds, from one end of heaven to the other.

³²"Now learn this parable from the fig tree: When its branch has already become tender and puts forth leaves, you know that summer is near. ³³So you also, when you see all these things, know that it is near—at the doors! ³⁴Assuredly, I say to you, this generation will by no means pass away till all these things take place. ³⁵Heaven and earth will pass away, but My words will by no means pass away.

³⁶"But of that day and hour no one knows, not even the angels of heaven, but My Father only. ³⁷But as the days of Noah were, so also will the coming of the Son of Man be. ³⁸For as in the days before the flood, they were eating and drinking, marrying and giving in marriage, until the day that Noah entered the ark, ³⁹and did not know until the flood came and took them all away, so also will the coming of the Son of Man be. ⁴⁰Then two men will be in the field: one will be taken and the other left. ⁴¹Two women will be grinding at the mill: one will be taken and the other left. ⁴²Watch therefore, for you do not know what hour your Lord is coming. ⁴³But know this, that if the master of the house had known what hour the thief would come, he would have watched and not allowed his house to be broken into. ⁴⁴Therefore you also be ready, for the Son of Man is coming at an hour you do not expect.

⁴⁵"Who then is a faithful and wise servant, whom his master made ruler over his household, to give them food in due season? ⁴⁶Blessed is that servant whom his master, when he comes, will find so doing. ⁴⁷Assuredly, I say to you that he will make him ruler over all his goods. ⁴⁸But if that evil servant says in his heart, 'My master is delaying his coming,' ⁴⁹and begins to beat his fellow servants, and to eat and drink with the drunkards, ⁵⁰the master of that servant will come on a day when he is not looking for him and at an hour that he is not aware of."

Matt 25:1-46 ¹"Then the kingdom of heaven shall be likened to ten virgins who took their lamps and went out to meet the bridegroom. ²Now five of them were wise, and five were foolish. ³Those who were foolish took their lamps and took no oil with them, ⁴but the wise took oil in their vessels with their lamps. ⁵But while the bridegroom was delayed, they all slumbered and slept.

⁶"And at midnight a cry was heard: 'Behold, the bridegroom is coming; go out to meet him!' ⁷Then all those virgins arose and trimmed their lamps. ⁸And the foolish said to the wise, 'Give us some of your oil, for our lamps are going out.' ⁹But the wise answered, saying, 'No, lest there should not be enough for us and you; but go rather to those who sell, and buy for yourselves.' ¹⁰And while they went to buy, the bridegroom came, and those who were ready went in with him to the wedding; and the door was shut.

¹¹"Afterward the other virgins came also, saying, 'Lord, Lord, open to us!' ¹²But he answered and said, 'Assuredly, I say to you, I do not know you.'

¹³"Watch therefore, for you know neither the day nor the hour in which the Son of Man is coming.

¹⁴"For the kingdom of heaven is like a man traveling to a far country, who called his own

servants and delivered his goods to them. ¹⁵And to one he gave five talents, to another two, and to another one, to each according to his own ability; and immediately he went on a journey. ¹⁶Then he who had received the five talents went and traded with them, and made another five talents. ¹⁷And likewise he who had received two gained two more also. ¹⁸But he who had received one went and dug in the ground, and hid his lord's money. ¹⁹After a long time the lord of those servants came and settled accounts with them.

²⁰"So he who had received five talents came and brought five other talents, saying, 'Lord, you delivered to me five talents; look, I have gained five more talents besides them.' ²¹His lord said to him, 'Well done, good and faithful servant; you were faithful over a few things, I will make you ruler over many things. Enter into the joy of your lord.' ²²He also who had received two talents came and said, 'Lord, you delivered to me two talents; look, I have gained two more talents besides them.' ²³His lord said to him, 'Well done, good and faithful servant; you have been faithful over a few things, I will make you ruler over many things. Enter into the joy of your lord.'

²⁴"Then he who had received the one talent came and said, 'Lord, I knew you to be a hard man, reaping where you have not sown, and gathering where you have not scattered seed. ²⁵And I was afraid, and went and hid your talent in the ground. Look, there you have what is yours.'

²⁶ "But his lord answered and said to him, 'You wicked and lazy servant, you knew that I reap where I have not sown, and gather where I have not scattered seed. ²⁷So you ought to have deposited my money with the bankers, and at my coming I would have received back my own with interest. ²⁸So take the talent from him, and give it to him who has ten talents.

²⁹ 'For to everyone who has, more will be given, and he will have abundance; but from him who does not have, even what he has will be taken away. ³⁰And cast the unprofitable servant into the outer darkness. There will be weeping and gnashing of teeth.'

³¹ "When the Son of Man comes in His glory, and all the holy angels with Him, then He will sit on the throne of His glory. ³²All the nations will be gathered before Him, and He will separate them one from another, as a shepherd divides his sheep from the goats. ³³And He will set the sheep on His right hand, but the goats on the left. ³⁴Then the King will say to those on His right hand, 'Come, you blessed of My Father, inherit the kingdom prepared for you from the foundation of the world: ³⁵for I was hungry and you gave Me food; I was thirsty and you gave Me drink; I was a stranger and you took Me in; ³⁶I was naked and you clothed Me; I was sick and you visited Me; I was in prison and you came to Me.'

³⁷ "Then the righteous will answer Him, saying, 'Lord, when did we see You hungry and feed You,

or thirsty and give You drink? ³⁸When did we see You a stranger and take You in, or naked and clothe You? ³⁹Or when did we see You sick, or in prison, and come to You?' ⁴⁰And the King will answer and say to them, 'Assuredly, I say to you, inasmuch as you did it to one of the least of these My brethren, you did it to Me.'

⁴¹"Then He will also say to those on the left hand, 'Depart from Me, you cursed, into the everlasting fire prepared for the devil and his angels: ⁴²for I was hungry and you gave Me no food; I was thirsty and you gave Me no drink; ⁴³I was a stranger and you did not take Me in, naked and you did not clothe Me, sick and in prison and you did not visit Me.'

⁴⁴"Then they also will answer Him, saying, 'Lord, when did we see You hungry or thirsty or a stranger or naked or sick or in prison, and did not minister to You?' ⁴⁵Then He will answer them, saying, 'Assuredly, I say to you, inasmuch as you did not do it to one of the least of these, you did not do it to Me.' ⁴⁶And these will go away into everlasting punishment, but the righteous into eternal life."

146. *A Plan to Kill the Messiah*

Matt 26:1-5 ¹Now it came to pass, when Jesus had finished all these sayings, that He said to His disciples, ²"You know that after two days is the Passover, and the Son of Man will be delivered up to be crucified."

³Then the chief priests, the scribes, and the

elders of the people assembled at the palace of the high priest, who was called Caiaphas, ⁴and plotted to take Jesus by trickery and kill Him. ⁵But they said, "Not during the feast, lest there be an uproar among the people."

147. A Good Deed by Mary

Jn 12:2-8 ²There they made Him a supper; and Martha served, but Lazarus was one of those who sat at the table with Him. ³Then Mary took a pound of very costly oil of spikenard, anointed the feet of Jesus, and wiped His feet with her hair. And the house was filled with the fragrance of the oil.

⁴But one of His disciples, Judas Iscariot, Simon's son, who would betray Him, said, ⁵"Why was this fragrant oil not sold for three hundred denarii and given to the poor?" ⁶This he said, not that he cared for the poor, but because he was a thief, and had the money box; and he used to take what was put in it.

⁷But Jesus said, "Let her alone; she has kept this for the day of My burial. ⁸For the poor you have with you always, but Me you do not have always."

Matt 26:12-13 ¹²"For in pouring this fragrant oil on My body, she did it for My burial. ¹³Assuredly, I say to you, wherever this gospel is preached in the whole world, what this woman has done will also be told as a memorial to her."

Lk 7:36-50 ³⁶Then one of the Pharisees asked Him to eat with him. And He went to the Pharisee's house, and sat down to eat. ³⁷And behold, a woman in the city who was a sinner, when she knew that Jesus sat at the table in the Pharisee's house, brought an alabaster flask of fragrant oil, ³⁸and stood at His feet behind Him weeping; and she began to wash His feet with her tears, and wiped them with the hair of her head; and she kissed His feet and anointed them with the fragrant oil. ³⁹Now when the Pharisee who had invited Him saw this, he spoke to himself, saying, "This Man, if He were a prophet, would know who and what manner of woman this is who is touching Him, for she is a sinner."

⁴⁰And Jesus answered and said to him, "Simon, I have something to say to you."

So he said, "Teacher, say it."

⁴¹"There was a certain creditor who had two debtors. One owed five hundred denarii, and the other fifty. ⁴²And when they had nothing with which to repay, he freely forgave them both. Tell Me, therefore, which of them will love him more?"

⁴³Simon answered and said, "I suppose the one whom he forgave more."

And He said to him, "You have rightly judged." ⁴⁴Then He turned to the woman and said to Simon, "Do you see this woman? I entered your house; you gave Me no water for My feet, but she has washed My feet with her tears and wiped them with the hair of her head. ⁴⁵You gave Me no kiss, but this woman has not ceased to kiss My feet since the time I came in. ⁴⁶You did not anoint My head with oil, but this woman has anointed My feet with fragrant oil. ⁴⁷Therefore I say to you, her sins, which are many, are forgiven, for she loved much. But to whom little is forgiven, the same loves little."

⁴⁸Then He said to her, "Your sins are forgiven."

⁴⁹And those who sat at the table with Him began to say to themselves, "Who is this who even forgives sins?"

⁵⁰Then He said to the woman, "Your faith has saved you. Go in peace."

148. Judas Plans to Betray Jesus

Lk 22:3-6 ³Then Satan entered Judas, surnamed Iscariot, who was numbered among the twelve. ⁴So he went his way and conferred with the chief priests and captains, how he might betray Him to them. ⁵And they were glad, and agreed to give him money. ⁶So he promised and sought opportunity to betray Him to them in the absence of the multitude.

A Religious Supper Becomes a Sacred Supper

149. The Passover Feast Is Arranged

Lk 22:7–13 ⁷Then came the Day of Unleavened Bread, when the Passover must be killed. ⁸And He sent Peter and John, saying, "Go and prepare the Passover for us, that we may eat."

⁹So they said to Him, "Where do You want us to prepare?"

¹⁰And He said to them, "Behold, when you have entered the city, a man will meet you carrying a pitcher of water; follow him into the house which he enters. ¹¹Then you shall say to the master of the house, 'The Teacher says to you, "Where is the guest room where I may eat the Passover with My disciples?"' ¹²Then he will show you a large, furnished upper room; there make ready."

¹³So they went and found it just as He had said to them, and they prepared the Passover.

Lk 22:14–16 ¹⁴When the hour had come, He sat down, and the twelve apostles with Him. ¹⁵Then He said to them, "With fervent desire I have desired to eat this Passover with you before I suffer; ¹⁶for I say to you, I will no longer eat of it until it is fulfilled in the kingdom of God."

Lk 22:24–30 ²⁴Now there was also a dispute among them, as to which of them should be considered the greatest. ²⁵And He said to them, "The kings of the Gentiles exercise lordship over them, and those who exercise authority over them are called 'benefactors.' ²⁶But not so among you; on the contrary, he who is greatest among you, let him be as the younger, and he who governs as he who serves. ²⁷For who is greater, he who sits at the table, or he who serves? Is it not he who sits at the table? Yet I am among you as the One who serves.

²⁸"But you are those who have continued with Me in My trials. ²⁹And I bestow upon you a kingdom, just as My Father bestowed one upon Me, ³⁰that you may eat and drink at My table in My kingdom, and sit on thrones judging the twelve tribes of Israel."

Jn 13:4–20 ⁴[Jesus] rose from supper and laid aside His garments, took a towel and girded Himself. ⁵After that, He poured water into a basin and began to wash the disciples' feet, and to wipe them with the towel with which He was girded. ⁶Then

He came to Simon Peter. And Peter said to Him, "Lord, are You washing my feet?"

⁷Jesus answered and said to him, "What I am doing you do not understand now, but you will know after this."

⁸Peter said to Him, "You shall never wash my feet!"

Jesus answered him, "If I do not wash you, you have no part with Me."

⁹Simon Peter said to Him, "Lord, not my feet only, but also my hands and my head!"

¹⁰Jesus said to him, "He who is bathed needs only to wash his feet, but is completely clean; and you are clean, but not all of you." ¹¹For He knew who would betray Him; therefore He said, "You are not all clean."

¹²So when He had washed their feet, taken His garments, and sat down again, He said to them, "Do you know what I have done to you? ¹³You call Me Teacher and Lord, and you say well, for so I am. ¹⁴If I then, your Lord and Teacher, have washed your feet, you also ought to wash one another's feet. ¹⁵For I have given you an example, that you should do as I have done to you. ¹⁶Most assuredly, I say to you, a servant is not greater than his master; nor is he who is sent greater than he who sent him. ¹⁷If you know these things, blessed are you if you do them.

¹⁸"I do not speak concerning all of you. I know whom I have chosen; but that the Scripture may be fulfilled, 'He who eats bread with Me has lifted up

his heel against Me.' ¹⁹Now I tell you before it comes, that when it does come to pass, you may believe that I am He. ²⁰Most assuredly, I say to you, he who receives whomever I send receives Me; and he who receives Me receives Him who sent Me."

151. A Second Chance for Judas

Lk 22:21-23 ²¹"But behold, the hand of My betrayer is with Me on the table. ²²And truly the Son of Man goes as it has been determined, but woe to that man by whom He is betrayed!"

²³Then they began to question among themselves, which of them it was who would do this thing.

Jn 13:23-26 ²³Now there was leaning on Jesus' bosom one of His disciples, whom Jesus loved. ²⁴Simon Peter therefore motioned to him to ask who it was of whom He spoke.

²⁵Then, leaning back on Jesus' breast, he said to Him, "Lord, who is it?"

²⁶Jesus answered, "It is he to whom I shall give a piece of bread when I have dipped it." And having dipped the bread, He gave it to Judas Iscariot, the son of Simon.

Matt 26:25 ²⁵Then Judas, who was betraying Him, answered and said, "Rabbi, is it I?"

Jn 13:27-30 ²⁷Now after the piece of bread, Satan entered him. Then Jesus said to him, "What you do, do quickly." ²⁸But no one at the table knew for what reason He said this to him. ²⁹For some thought, because Judas had the money box, that

~ 216 ~

Jesus had said to him, "Buy those things we need for the feast," or that he should give something to the poor.

³⁰Having received the piece of bread, he then went out immediately. And it was night.

152. Significance of the Lord's Supper

Mk 14:22-25 ²²And as they were eating, Jesus took bread, blessed and broke it, and gave it to them and said, "Take, eat; this is My body."

²³Then He took the cup, and when He had given thanks He gave it to them, and they all drank from it. ²⁴And He said to them, "This is My blood of the new covenant, which is shed for many. ²⁵Assuredly, I say to you, I will no longer drink of the fruit of the vine until that day when I drink it new in the kingdom of God."

153. Final Observations Shared with Disciples

Jn 13:33-38 ³³"Little children, I shall be with you a little while longer. You will seek Me; and as I said to the Jews, 'Where I am going, you cannot come,' so now I say to you. ³⁴A new commandment I give to you, that you love one another; as I have loved you, that you also love one another. ³⁵By this all will know that you are My disciples, if you have love for one another."

³⁶Simon Peter said to Him, "Lord, where are You going?"

Jesus answered him, "Where I am going you

cannot follow Me now, but you shall follow Me afterward."

³⁷Peter said to Him, "Lord, why can I not follow You now? I will lay down my life for Your sake."

³⁸Jesus answered him, "Will you lay down your life for My sake? Most assuredly, I say to you, the rooster shall not crow till you have denied Me three times."

Matt 26:31-33 ³¹Then Jesus said to them, "All of you will be made to stumble because of Me this night, for it is written:

> 'I will strike the Shepherd,
>   And the sheep of the flock will be
>   scattered.'

³²But after I have been raised, I will go before you to Galilee."

³³Peter answered and said to Him, "Even if all are made to stumble because of You, I will never be made to stumble."

Lk 22:31-38 ³¹And the Lord said, "Simon, Simon! Indeed, Satan has asked for you, that he may sift you as wheat. ³²But I have prayed for you, that your faith should not fail; and when you have returned to Me, strengthen your brethren."

³³But he said to Him, "Lord, I am ready to go with You, both to prison and to death."

³⁴Then He said, "I tell you, Peter, the rooster

shall not crow this day before you will deny three times that you know Me."

³⁵And He said to them, "When I sent you without money bag, knapsack, and sandals, did you lack anything?"

So they said, "Nothing."

³⁶Then He said to them, "But now, he who has a money bag, let him take it, and likewise a knapsack; and he who has no sword, let him sell his garment and buy one. ³⁷For I say to you that this which is written must still be accomplished in Me: 'And He was numbered with the transgressors.' For the things concerning Me have an end."

³⁸So they said, "Lord, look, here are two swords."

And He said to them, "It is enough."

154. *Jesus and Death: He Will Return*

Jn 14:1–30 ¹"Let not your heart be troubled; you believe in God, believe also in Me. ²In My Father's house are many mansions; if it were not so, I would have told you. I go to prepare a place for you. ³And if I go and prepare a place for you, I will come again and receive you to Myself; that where I am, there you may be also. ⁴And where I go you know, and the way you know."

⁵Thomas said to Him, "Lord, we do not know where You are going, and how can we know the way?"

⁶Jesus said to him, "I am the way, the truth,

and the life. No one comes to the Father except through Me.

7 "If you had known Me, you would have known My Father also; and from now on you know Him and have seen Him."

8 Philip said to Him, "Lord, show us the Father, and it is sufficient for us."

9 Jesus said to him, "Have I been with you so long, and yet you have not known Me, Philip? He who has seen Me has seen the Father; so how can you say, 'Show us the Father'? 10 Do you not believe that I am in the Father, and the Father in Me? The words that I speak to you I do not speak on My own authority; but the Father who dwells in Me does the works. 11 Believe Me that I am in the Father and the Father in Me, or else believe Me for the sake of the works themselves.

12 "Most assuredly, I say to you, he who believes in Me, the works that I do he will do also; and greater works than these he will do, because I go to My Father. 13 And whatever you ask in My name, that I will do, that the Father may be glorified in the Son. 14 If you ask anything in My name, I will do it.

15 "If you love Me, keep My commandments. 16 And I will pray the Father, and He will give you another Helper, that He may abide with you forever— 17 the Spirit of truth, whom the world cannot receive, because it neither sees Him nor knows Him; but you know Him, for He dwells with you and will be in you. 18 I will not leave you orphans; I will come to you.

¹⁹"A little while longer and the world will see Me no more, but you will see Me. Because I live, you will live also. ²⁰At that day you will know that I am in My Father, and you in Me, and I in you. ²¹He who has My commandments and keeps them, it is he who loves Me. And he who loves Me will be loved by My Father, and I will love him and manifest Myself to him."

²²Judas (not Iscariot) said to Him, "Lord, how is it that You will manifest Yourself to us, and not to the world?"

²³Jesus answered and said to him, "If anyone loves Me, he will keep My word; and My Father will love him, and We will come to him and make Our home with him. ²⁴He who does not love Me does not keep My words; and the word which you hear is not Mine but the Father's who sent Me.

²⁵"These things I have spoken to you while being present with you. ²⁶But the Helper, the Holy Spirit, whom the Father will send in My name, He will teach you all things, and bring to your remembrance all things that I said to you. ²⁷Peace I leave with you, My peace I give to you; not as the world gives do I give to you. Let not your heart be troubled, neither let it be afraid. ²⁸You have heard Me say to you, 'I am going away and coming back to you.' If you loved Me, you would rejoice because I said, 'I am going to the Father,' for My Father is greater than I.

²⁹"And now I have told you before it comes, that when it does come to pass, you may believe.

³⁰I will no longer talk much with you, for the ruler of this world is coming, and he has nothing in Me."

155. Last Walk to the Garden

Mk 14:26 ²⁶And when they had sung a hymn, they went out to the Mount of Olives.

Jn 15:1–27 ¹"I am the true vine, and My Father is the vinedresser. ²Every branch in Me that does not bear fruit He takes away; and every branch that bears fruit He prunes, that it may bear more fruit. ³You are already clean because of the word which I have spoken to you. ⁴Abide in Me, and I in you. As the branch cannot bear fruit of itself, unless it abides in the vine, neither can you, unless you abide in Me.

⁵"I am the vine, you are the branches. He who abides in Me, and I in him, bears much fruit; for without Me you can do nothing. ⁶If anyone does not abide in Me, he is cast out as a branch and is withered; and they gather them and throw them into the fire, and they are burned. ⁷If you abide in Me, and My words abide in you, you will ask what you desire, and it shall be done for you. ⁸By this My Father is glorified, that you bear much fruit; so you will be My disciples.

⁹"As the Father loved Me, I also have loved you; abide in My love. ¹⁰If you keep My commandments, you will abide in My love, just as I have kept My Father's commandments and abide in His love.

¹¹"These things I have spoken to you, that My joy may remain in you, and that your joy may be

full. [12]This is My commandment, that you love one another as I have loved you. [13]Greater love has no one than this, than to lay down one's life for his friends. [14]You are My friends if you do whatever I command you. [15]No longer do I call you servants, for a servant does not know what his master is doing; but I have called you friends, for all things that I heard from My Father I have made known to you. [16]You did not choose Me, but I chose you and appointed you that you should go and bear fruit, and that your fruit should remain, that whatever you ask the Father in My name He may give you. [17]These things I command you, that you love one another.

[18]"If the world hates you, you know that it hated Me before it hated you. [19]If you were of the world, the world would love its own. Yet because you are not of the world, but I chose you out of the world, therefore the world hates you. [20]Remember the word that I said to you, 'A servant is not greater than his master.' If they persecuted Me, they will also persecute you. If they kept My word, they will keep yours also. [21]But all these things they will do to you for My name's sake, because they do not know Him who sent Me. [22]If I had not come and spoken to them, they would have no sin, but now they have no excuse for their sin. [23]He who hates Me hates My Father also. [24]If I had not done among them the works which no one else did, they would have no sin; but now they have seen and also hated both Me and My Father. [25]But this happened that

the word might be fulfilled which is written in their law, 'They hated Me without a cause.'

²⁶"But when the Helper comes, whom I shall send to you from the Father, the Spirit of truth who proceeds from the Father, He will testify of Me. ²⁷And you also will bear witness, because you have been with Me from the beginning."

156. More Instructions to His Disciples

Jn 16:1-33 ¹"These things I have spoken to you, that you should not be made to stumble. ²They will put you out of the synagogues; yes, the time is coming that whoever kills you will think that he offers God service. ³And these things they will do to you because they have not known the Father nor Me. ⁴But these things I have told you, that when the time comes, you may remember that I told you of them.

"And these things I did not say to you at the beginning, because I was with you.

⁵"But now I go away to Him who sent Me, and none of you asks Me, 'Where are You going?' ⁶But because I have said these things to you, sorrow has filled your heart. ⁷Nevertheless I tell you the truth. It is to your advantage that I go away; for if I do not go away, the Helper will not come to you; but if I depart, I will send Him to you. ⁸And when He has come, He will convict the world of sin, and of righteousness, and of judgment: ⁹of sin, because they do not believe in Me; ¹⁰of righteousness, be-

cause I go to My Father and you see Me no more; [11] of judgment, because the ruler of this world is judged.

[12] "I still have many things to say to you, but you cannot bear them now. [13] However, when He, the Spirit of truth, has come, He will guide you into all truth; for He will not speak on His own authority, but whatever He hears He will speak; and He will tell you things to come. [14] He will glorify Me, for He will take of what is Mine and declare it to you. [15] All things that the Father has are Mine. Therefore I said that He will take of Mine and declare it to you.

[16] "A little while, and you will not see Me; and again a little while, and you will see Me, because I go to the Father."

[17] Then some of His disciples said among themselves, "What is this that He says to us, 'A little while, and you will not see Me; and again a little while, and you will see Me'; and, 'because I go to the Father'?" [18] They said therefore, "What is this that He says, 'A little while'? We do not know what He is saying."

[19] Now Jesus knew that they desired to ask Him, and He said to them, "Are you inquiring among yourselves about what I said, 'A little while, and you will not see Me; and again a little while, and you will see Me'? [20] Most assuredly, I say to you that you will weep and lament, but the world will rejoice; and you will be sorrowful, but your sorrow will be turned into joy. [21] A woman, when she is in labor, has sorrow because her hour has come; but

as soon as she has given birth to the child, she no longer remembers the anguish, for joy that a human being has been born into the world. ²²Therefore you now have sorrow; but I will see you again and your heart will rejoice, and your joy no one will take from you.

²³"And in that day you will ask Me nothing. Most assuredly, I say to you, whatever you ask the Father in My name He will give you. ²⁴Until now you have asked nothing in My name. Ask, and you will receive, that your joy may be full.

²⁵"These things I have spoken to you in figurative language; but the time is coming when I will no longer speak to you in figurative language, but I will tell you plainly about the Father. ²⁶In that day you will ask in My name, and I do not say to you that I shall pray the Father for you; ²⁷for the Father Himself loves you, because you have loved Me, and have believed that I came forth from God. ²⁸I came forth from the Father and have come into the world. Again, I leave the world and go to the Father."

²⁹His disciples said to Him, "See, now You are speaking plainly, and using no figure of speech! ³⁰Now we are sure that You know all things, and have no need that anyone should question You. By this we believe that You came forth from God."

³¹Jesus answered them, "Do you now believe? ³²Indeed the hour is coming, yes, has now come, that you will be scattered, each to his own, and will leave Me alone. And yet I am not alone, because

the Father is with Me. ³³These things I have spoken to you, that in Me you may have peace. In the world you will have tribulation; but be of good cheer, I have overcome the world."

157. Christ's Great Intercessory Prayer

Jn 17:1-26 ¹Jesus spoke these words, lifted up His eyes to heaven, and said: "Father, the hour has come. Glorify Your Son, that Your Son also may glorify You, ²as You have given Him authority over all flesh, that He should give eternal life to as many as You have given Him. ³And this is eternal life, that they may know You, the only true God, and Jesus Christ whom You have sent. ⁴I have glorified You on the earth. I have finished the work which You have given Me to do. ⁵And now, O Father, glorify Me together with Yourself, with the glory which I had with You before the world was.

⁶"I have manifested Your name to the men whom You have given Me out of the world. They were Yours, You gave them to Me, and they have kept Your word. ⁷Now they have known that all things which You have given Me are from You. ⁸For I have given to them the words which You have given Me; and they have received them, and have known surely that I came forth from You; and they have believed that You sent Me.

⁹"I pray for them. I do not pray for the world but for those whom You have given Me, for they are Yours. ¹⁰And all Mine are Yours, and Yours are Mine, and I am glorified in them. ¹¹Now I am no

longer in the world, but these are in the world, and I come to You. Holy Father, keep through Your name those whom You have given Me, that they may be one as We are. [12]While I was with them in the world, I kept them in Your name. Those whom You gave Me I have kept; and none of them is lost except the son of perdition, that the Scripture might be fulfilled. [13]But now I come to You, and these things I speak in the world, that they may have My joy fulfilled in themselves. [14]I have given them Your word; and the world has hated them because they are not of the world, just as I am not of the world. [15]I do not pray that You should take them out of the world, but that You should keep them from the evil one. [16]They are not of the world, just as I am not of the world. [17]Sanctify them by Your truth. Your word is truth. [18]As You sent Me into the world, I also have sent them into the world. [19]And for their sakes I sanctify Myself, that they also may be sanctified by the truth.

[20]"I do not pray for these alone, but also for those who will believe in Me through their word; [21]that they all may be one, as You, Father, are in Me, and I in You; that they also may be one in Us, that the world may believe that You sent Me. [22]And the glory which You gave Me I have given them, that they may be one just as We are one: [23]I in them, and You in Me; that they may be made perfect in one, and that the world may know that You have sent Me, and have loved them as You have loved Me.

²⁴"Father, I desire that they also whom You gave Me may be with Me where I am, that they may behold My glory which You have given Me; for You loved Me before the foundation of the world. ²⁵O righteous Father! The world has not known You, but I have known You; and these have known that You sent Me. ²⁶And I have declared to them Your name, and will declare it, that the love with which You loved Me may be in them, and I in them "

JESUS TAKEN CAPTIVE
IN GETHSEMANE

158. Moments of Agony in the Garden

Matt 26:36-39 ³⁶Then Jesus came with them to a place called Gethsemane, and said to the disciples, "Sit here while I go and pray over there." ³⁷And He took with Him Peter and the two sons of Zebedee, and He began to be sorrowful and deeply distressed. ³⁸Then He said to them, "My soul is exceedingly sorrowful, even to death. Stay here and watch with Me."

³⁹He went a little farther and fell on His face, and prayed, saying, "O My Father, if it is possible, let this cup pass from Me; nevertheless, not as I will, but as You will."

Lk 22:42-44 ⁴²"Father, if it is Your will, take this cup away from Me; nevertheless not My will, but Yours, be done." ⁴³Then an angel appeared to Him from heaven, strengthening Him. ⁴⁴And being in agony, He prayed more earnestly. Then His sweat

became like great drops of blood falling down to the ground.

Mk 14:37-42 ³⁷Then He came and found them sleeping, and said to Peter, "Simon, are you sleeping? Could you not watch one hour? ³⁸Watch and pray, lest you enter into temptation. The spirit indeed is willing, but the flesh is weak."

³⁹Again He went away and prayed, and spoke the same words. ⁴⁰And when He returned, He found them asleep again, for their eyes were heavy; and they did not know what to answer Him.

⁴¹Then He came the third time and said to them, "Are you still sleeping and resting? It is enough! The hour has come; behold, the Son of Man is being betrayed into the hands of sinners. ⁴²Rise, let us be going. See, My betrayer is at hand."

159. The Lord Betrayed and Arrested

Jn 18:2-3 ²And Judas, who betrayed Him, also knew the place; for Jesus often met there with His disciples. ³Then Judas, having received a detachment of troops, and officers from the chief priests and Pharisees, came there with lanterns, torches, and weapons.

Mk 14:44-45 ⁴⁴Now His betrayer had given them a signal, saying, "Whomever I kiss, He is the One; seize Him and lead Him away safely."

⁴⁵As soon as he had come, immediately he went up to Him and said to Him, "Rabbi, Rabbi!" and kissed Him.

Lk 22:48 [48] "But Jesus said to him, "Judas, are you betraying the Son of Man with a kiss?"

Jn 18:4–9 [4] Jesus therefore, knowing all things that would come upon Him, went forward and said to them, "Whom are you seeking?"

[5] They answered Him, "Jesus of Nazareth."

Jesus said to them, "I am He." And Judas, who betrayed Him, also stood with them. [6] Now when He said to them, "I am He," they drew back and fell to the ground.

[7] Then He asked them again, "Whom are you seeking?"

And they said, "Jesus of Nazareth."

[8] Jesus answered, "I have told you that I am He. Therefore, if you seek Me, let these go their way," [9] that the saying might be fulfilled which He spoke, "Of those whom You gave Me I have lost none."

Lk 22:49 [49] When those around Him saw what was going to happen, they said to Him, "Lord, shall we strike with the sword?"

Jn 18:10–11 [10] Then Simon Peter, having a sword, drew it and struck the high priest's servant, and cut off his right ear. The servant's name was Malchus.

[11] So Jesus said to Peter, "Put your sword into the sheath. Shall I not drink the cup which My Father has given Me?"

Matt 26:53–54 [53] "Or do you think that I cannot now pray to My Father, and He will provide Me with more than twelve legions of angels? [54] How then could the Scriptures be fulfilled, that it must happen thus?"

Lk 22:52-53 ⁵²Then Jesus said to the chief priests, captains of the temple, and the elders who had come to Him, "Have you come out, as against a robber, with swords and clubs? ⁵³When I was with you daily in the temple, you did not try to seize Me. But this is your hour, and the power of darkness."

Matt 26:56 ⁵⁶"But all this was done that the Scriptures of the prophets might be fulfilled."

Then all the disciples forsook Him and fled.

Jn 18:12 ¹²Then the detachment of troops and the captain and the officers of the Jews arrested Jesus and bound Him.

Mk 14:51-52 ⁵¹Now a certain young man followed Him, having a linen cloth thrown around his naked body. And the young men laid hold of him, ⁵²and he left the linen cloth and fled from them naked.

160. Annas Starts the Trial of Jesus

Jn 18:13-14 ¹³And they led Him away to Annas first, for he was the father-in-law of Caiaphas who was high priest that year. ¹⁴Now it was Caiaphas who advised the Jews that it was expedient that one man should die for the people.

Jn 18:19-23 ¹⁹The high priest then asked Jesus about His disciples and His doctrine.

²⁰Jesus answered him, "I spoke openly to the world. I always taught in synagogues and in the temple, where the Jews always meet, and in secret I have said nothing. ²¹Why do you ask Me? Ask

those who have heard Me what I said to them. Indeed they know what I said."

²²And when He had said these things, one of the officers who stood by struck Jesus with the palm of his hand, saying, "Do You answer the high priest like that?"

²³Jesus answered him, "If I have spoken evil, bear witness of the evil; but if well, why do you strike Me?"

161. Peter and John Follow from a Distance

Jn 18:15–18 ¹⁵And Simon Peter followed Jesus, and so did another disciple. Now that disciple was known to the high priest, and went with Jesus into the courtyard of the high priest. ¹⁶But Peter stood at the door outside. Then the other disciple, who was known to the high priest, went out and spoke to her who kept the door, and brought Peter in. ¹⁷Then the servant girl who kept the door said to Peter, "You are not also one of this Man's disciples, are you?"

He said, "I am not."

¹⁸Now the servants and officers who had made a fire of coals stood there, for it was cold, and they warmed themselves. And Peter stood with them and warmed himself.

162. An Unfair Trial Gains Momentum

Matt 26:57–68 ⁵⁷And those who had laid hold of Jesus led Him away to Caiaphas the high priest, where the scribes and the elders were assembled. ⁵⁸But Peter followed Him at a distance to the high priest's courtyard. And he went in and sat with the servants to see the end.

⁵⁹Now the chief priests, the elders, and all the council sought false testimony against Jesus to put Him to death, ⁶⁰but found none. Even though many false witnesses came forward, they found none. But at last two false witnesses came forward ⁶¹and said, "This fellow said, 'I am able to destroy the temple of God and to build it in three days.'"

⁶²And the high priest arose and said to Him, "Do You answer nothing? What is it these men testify against You?" ⁶³But Jesus kept silent. And the high priest answered and said to Him, "I put You under oath by the living God: Tell us if You are the Christ, the Son of God!"

⁶⁴Jesus said to him, "It is as you said. Nevertheless, I say to you, hereafter you will see the Son of Man sitting at the right hand of the Power, and coming on the clouds of heaven."

⁶⁵Then the high priest tore his clothes, saying, "He has spoken blasphemy! What further need do we have of witnesses? Look, now you have heard His blasphemy! ⁶⁶What do you think?"

They answered and said, "He is deserving of death."

⁶⁷Then they spat in His face and beat Him; and others struck Him with the palms of their hands, ⁶⁸saying, "Prophesy to us, Christ! Who is the one who struck You?"

Lk 22:65 "And many other things they blasphemously spoke against Him.

163. Peter Refuses to Know Jesus

Mk 14:66-72 [66]Now as Peter was below in the courtyard, one of the servant girls of the high priest came. [67]And when she saw Peter warming himself, she looked at him and said, "You also were with Jesus of Nazareth."

[68]But he denied it, saying, "I neither know nor understand what you are saying." And he went out on the porch, and a rooster crowed.

[69]And the servant girl saw him again, and began to say to those who stood by, "This is one of them." [70]But he denied it again.

And a little later those who stood by said to Peter again, "Surely you are one of them; for you are a Galilean, and your speech shows it."

[71]Then he began to curse and swear, "I do not know this Man of whom you speak!"

[72]A second time the rooster crowed. Then Peter called to mind the word that Jesus had said to him, "Before the rooster crows twice, you will deny Me three times." And when he thought about it, he wept.

164. The Sanhedrin Adds Condemnation

Lk 22:66-71 [66]As soon as it was day, the elders of the people, both chief priests and scribes, came together and led Him into their council, saying, 67 "If You are the Christ, tell us."

But He said to them, "If I tell you, you will by no means believe. 68 And if I also ask you, you will by no means answer Me or let Me go. 69 Hereafter the Son of Man will sit on the right hand of the power of God."

70 Then they all said, "Are You then the Son of God?"

So He said to them, "You rightly say that I am."

71 And they said, "What further testimony do we need? For we have heard it ourselves from His own mouth."

165. A Betrayer Hangs Himself

Matt 27:3–10 ³ Then Judas, His betrayer, seeing that He had been condemned, was remorseful and brought back the thirty pieces of silver to the chief priests and elders, ⁴ saying, "I have sinned by betraying innocent blood."

And they said, "What is that to us? You see to it!"

⁵ Then he threw down the pieces of silver in the temple and departed, and went and hanged himself.

⁶ But the chief priests took the silver pieces and said, "It is not lawful to put them into the treasury, because they are the price of blood." ⁷ And they consulted together and bought with them the potter's

field, to bury strangers in. ⁸Therefore that field has been called the Field of Blood to this day.

⁹Then was fulfilled what was spoken by Jeremiah the prophet, saying, "And they took the thirty pieces of silver, the value of Him who was priced, whom they of the children of Israel priced, ¹⁰and gave them for the potter's field, as the LORD directed me."

166. Pilate Enters the Trial Proceedings

Jn 18:28–30 ²⁸Then they led Jesus from Caiaphas to the Praetorium, and it was early morning. But they themselves did not go into the Praetorium, lest they should be defiled, but that they might eat the Passover. ²⁹Pilate then went out to them and said, "What accusation do you bring against this Man?"

³⁰They answered and said to him, "If He were not an evildoer, we would not have delivered Him up to you."

Lk 23:2–3 ²And they began to accuse Him, saying, "We found this fellow perverting the nation, and forbidding to pay taxes to Caesar, saying that He Himself is Christ, a King."

³Then Pilate asked Him, saying, "Are You the King of the Jews?"

He answered him and said, "It is as you say."

Matt 27:12–14 ¹²And while He was being accused by the chief priests and elders, He answered nothing.

¹³Then Pilate said to Him, "Do You not hear

how many things they testify against You?" ¹⁴But He answered him not one word, so that the governor marveled greatly.

_{Jn 18:31-38} ³¹Then Pilate said to them, "You take Him and judge Him according to your law."

Therefore the Jews said to him, "It is not lawful for us to put anyone to death," ³²that the saying of Jesus might be fulfilled which He spoke, signifying by what death He would die.

³³Then Pilate entered the Praetorium again, called Jesus, and said to Him, "Are You the King of the Jews?"

³⁴Jesus answered him, "Are you speaking for yourself about this, or did others tell you this concerning Me?"

³⁵Pilate answered, "Am I a Jew? Your own nation and the chief priests have delivered You to me. What have You done?"

³⁶Jesus answered, "My kingdom is not of this world. If My kingdom were of this world, My servants would fight, so that I should not be delivered to the Jews; but now My kingdom is not from here."

³⁷Pilate therefore said to Him, "Are You a king then?"

Jesus answered, "You say rightly that I am a king. For this cause I was born, and for this cause I have come into the world, that I should bear witness to the truth. Everyone who is of the truth hears My voice."

³⁸Pilate said to Him, "What is truth?" And

when he had said this, he went out again to the Jews, and said to them, "I find no fault in Him at all."

Lk 23:5-7 [5]But they were the more fierce, saying, "He stirs up the people, teaching throughout all Judea, beginning from Galilee to this place."

[6]When Pilate heard of Galilee, he asked if the Man were a Galilean. [7]And as soon as he knew that He belonged to Herod's jurisdiction, he sent Him to Herod, who was also in Jerusalem at that time.

167. The Ordeal with Herod Antipas

Lk 23:8-12 [8]Now when Herod saw Jesus, he was exceedingly glad; for he had desired for a long time to see Him, because he had heard many things about Him, and he hoped to see some miracle done by Him. [9]Then he questioned Him with many words, but He answered him nothing. [10]And the chief priests and scribes stood and vehemently accused Him. [11]Then Herod, with his men of war, treated Him with contempt and mocked Him, arrayed Him in a gorgeous robe, and sent Him back to Pilate. [12]That very day Pilate and Herod became friends with each other, for previously they had been at enmity with each other.

168. Before Pilate Once More

Lk 23:13-16 [13]Then Pilate, when he had called together the chief priests, the rulers, and the people, [14]said to them, "You have brought this Man to me, as one who misleads the people. And indeed, having examined Him in your presence, I have found no fault in this Man concerning those things of which you accuse Him; ¹⁵no, neither did Herod, for I sent you back to him; and indeed nothing deserving of death has been done by Him. ¹⁶I will therefore chastise Him and release Him."

Matt 27:15–23 ¹⁵Now at the feast the governor was accustomed to releasing to the multitude one prisoner whom they wished. ¹⁶And at that time they had a notorious prisoner called Barabbas. ¹⁷Therefore, when they had gathered together, Pilate said to them, "Whom do you want me to release to you? Barabbas, or Jesus who is called Christ?" ¹⁸For he knew that they had handed Him over because of envy.

¹⁹While he was sitting on the judgment seat, his wife sent to him, saying, "Have nothing to do with that just Man, for I have suffered many things today in a dream because of Him."

²⁰But the chief priests and elders persuaded the multitudes that they should ask for Barabbas and destroy Jesus. ²¹The governor answered and said to them, "Which of the two do you want me to release to you?"

They said, "Barabbas!"

²²Pilate said to them, "What then shall I do with Jesus who is called Christ?"

They all said to him, "Let Him be crucified!"

²³Then the governor said, "Why, what evil has He done?"

But they cried out all the more, saying, "Let Him be crucified!"

Lk 23:20–23 20Pilate, therefore, wishing to release Jesus, again called out to them. 21But they shouted, saying, "Crucify Him, crucify Him!"

22Then he said to them the third time, "Why, what evil has He done? I have found no reason for death in Him. I will therefore chastise Him and let Him go."

23But they were insistent, demanding with loud voices that He be crucified. And the voices of these men and of the chief priests prevailed.

Matt 27:24–30 24When Pilate saw that he could not prevail at all, but rather that a tumult was rising, he took water and washed his hands before the multitude, saying, "I am innocent of the blood of this just Person. You see to it."

25And all the people answered and said, "His blood be on us and on our children."

26Then he released Barabbas to them; and when he had scourged Jesus, he delivered Him to be crucified.

27Then the soldiers of the governor took Jesus into the Praetorium and gathered the whole garrison around Him. 28And they stripped Him and put a scarlet robe on Him. 29When they had twisted a crown of thorns, they put it on His head, and a reed in His right hand. And they bowed the knee before Him and mocked Him, saying, "Hail, King of the Jews!" 30Then they spat on Him, and took the reed and struck Him on the head.

Jn 19:4–16 ⁴Pilate then went out again, and said to them, "Behold, I am bringing Him out to you, that you may know that I find no fault in Him."

⁵Then Jesus came out, wearing the crown of thorns and the purple robe. And Pilate said to them, "Behold the Man!"

⁶Therefore, when the chief priests and officers saw Him, they cried out, saying, "Crucify Him, crucify Him!"

Pilate said to them, "You take Him and crucify Him, for I find no fault in Him."

⁷The Jews answered him, "We have a law, and according to our law He ought to die, because He made Himself the Son of God."

⁸Therefore, when Pilate heard that saying, he was the more afraid, ⁹and went again into the Praetorium, and said to Jesus, "Where are You from?" But Jesus gave him no answer.

¹⁰Then Pilate said to Him, "Are You not speaking to me? Do You not know that I have power to crucify You, and power to release You?"

¹¹Jesus answered, "You could have no power at all against Me unless it had been given you from above. Therefore the one who delivered Me to you has the greater sin."

¹²From then on Pilate sought to release Him, but the Jews cried out, saying, "If you let this Man go, you are not Caesar's friend. Whoever makes himself a king speaks against Caesar."

¹³When Pilate therefore heard that saying, he brought Jesus out and sat down in the judgment

seat in a place that is called The Pavement, but in Hebrew, Gabbatha. ¹⁴Now it was the Preparation Day of the Passover, and about the sixth hour. And he said to the Jews, "Behold your King!"

¹⁵But they cried out, "Away with Him, away with Him! Crucify Him!"

Pilate said to them, "Shall I crucify your King?"

The chief priests answered, "We have no king but Caesar!"

¹⁶Then he delivered Him to them to be crucified. Then they took Jesus and led Him away.

Mk 15:20 ²⁰And when they had mocked Him, they took the purple off Him, put His own clothes on Him, and led Him out to crucify Him.

THAT DAY AT CALVARY

169. The Difficult Road to Death

Jn 19:17 ¹⁷And He, bearing His cross, went out to a place called the Place of a Skull, which is called in Hebrew, Golgotha.

Lk 23:26-32 ²⁶Now as they led Him away, they laid hold of a certain man, Simon a Cyrenian, who was coming from the country, and on him they laid the cross that he might bear it after Jesus.

²⁷And a great multitude of the people followed Him, and women who also mourned and lamented Him. ²⁸But Jesus, turning to them, said, "Daughters of Jerusalem, do not weep for Me, but weep for yourselves and for your children. ²⁹For indeed the days are coming in which they will say, 'Blessed are the barren, wombs that never bore, and breasts which never nursed!' ³⁰Then they will begin 'to say to the mountains, "Fall on us!" and to the hills, "Cover us!" ³¹For if they do these things in the green wood, what will be done in the dry?"

³³There were also two others, criminals, led with Him to be put to death.

170. "And There They Crucified Him"

Mk 15:22-25 ²²And they brought Him to the place Golgotha, which is translated, Place of a Skull. ²³Then they gave Him wine mingled with myrrh to drink, but He did not take it. ²⁴And when they crucified Him, they divided His garments, casting lots for them to determine what every man should take.

²⁵Now it was the third hour, and they crucified Him.

Jn 19:18-24 ¹⁸[T]hey crucified Him, and two others with Him, one on either side, and Jesus in the center. ¹⁹Now Pilate wrote a title and put it on the cross. And the writing was:

JESUS OF NAZARETH,
THE KING OF THE JEWS.

²⁰Then many of the Jews read this title, for the place where Jesus was crucified was near the city; and it was written in Hebrew, Greek, and Latin.

²¹Therefore the chief priests of the Jews said to Pilate, "Do not write, 'The King of the Jews,' but, 'He said, "I am the King of the Jews."'"

²²Pilate answered, "What I have written, I have written."

²³Then the soldiers, when they had crucified Jesus, took His garments and made four parts, to each soldier a part, and also the tunic. Now the

tunic was without seam, woven from the top in one piece. ²⁴They said therefore among themselves, "Let us not tear it, but cast lots for it, whose it shall be," that the Scripture might be fulfilled which says:

"They divided My garments among them,
And for My clothing they cast lots."

Therefore the soldiers did these things.

Matt 27:36-43 ³⁶Sitting down, they kept watch over Him there. ³⁷And they put up over His head the accusation written against Him:

THIS IS JESUS THE KING OF THE JEWS.

³⁸Then two robbers were crucified with Him, one on the right and another on the left.

³⁹And those who passed by blasphemed Him, wagging their heads ⁴⁰and saying, "You who destroy the temple and build it in three days, save Yourself! If You are the Son of God, come down from the cross."

⁴¹Likewise the chief priests also, mocking with the scribes and elders, said, ⁴²"He saved others; Himself He cannot save. If He is the King of Israel, let Him now come down from the cross, and we will believe Him. ⁴³He trusted in God; let Him deliver Him now if He will have Him; for He said, 'I am the Son of God.'"

Lk 23:36-43 ³⁶The soldiers also mocked Him, coming and offering Him sour wine, ³⁷and saying, "If You are the King of the Jews, save Yourself."

³⁸And an inscription also was written over Him in letters of Greek, Latin, and Hebrew:

THIS IS THE KING OF THE JEWS.

³⁹Then one of the criminals who were hanged blasphemed Him, saying, "If You are the Christ, save Yourself and us."

⁴⁰But the other, answering, rebuked him, saying, "Do you not even fear God, seeing you are under the same condemnation? ⁴¹And we indeed justly, for we receive the due reward of our deeds; but this Man has done nothing wrong." ⁴²Then he said to Jesus, "Lord, remember me when You come into Your kingdom."

⁴³And Jesus said to him, "Assuredly, I say to you, today you will be with Me in Paradise."

Jn 19:25–27 ²⁵Now there stood by the cross of Jesus His mother, and His mother's sister, Mary the wife of Clopas, and Mary Magdalene. ²⁶When Jesus therefore saw His mother, and the disciple whom He loved standing by, He said to His mother, "Woman, behold your son!" ²⁷Then He said to the disciple, "Behold your mother!" And from that hour that disciple took her to his own home.

Lk 23:44 ⁴⁴Now it was about the sixth hour, and there was darkness over all the earth until the ninth hour.

Mk 15:34–37 ³⁴And at the ninth hour Jesus cried out with a loud voice, saying, "Eloi, Eloi, lama sabachthani?" which is translated, "My God, My God, why have You forsaken Me?"

³⁵Some of those who stood by, when they heard that, said, "Look, He is calling for Elijah!" ³⁶Then someone ran and filled a sponge full of sour wine, put it on a reed, and offered it to Him to drink, saying, "Let Him alone; let us see if Elijah will come to take Him down."

³⁷And Jesus cried out with a loud voice, and breathed His last.

Matt 27:51-54 ⁵¹Then, behold, the veil of the temple was torn in two from top to bottom; and the earth quaked, and the rocks were split, ⁵²and the graves were opened; and many bodies of the saints who had fallen asleep were raised; ⁵³and coming out of the graves after His resurrection, they went into the holy city and appeared to many.

⁵⁴So when the centurion and those with him, who were guarding Jesus, saw the earthquake and the things that had happened, they feared greatly, saying, "Truly this was the Son of God!"

Mk 15:40-41 ⁴⁰There were also women looking on from afar, among whom were Mary Magdalene, Mary the mother of James the Less and of Joses, and Salome, ⁴¹who also followed Him and ministered to Him when He was in Galilee, and many other women who came up with Him to Jerusalem.

Jn 19:31-37 ³¹Therefore, because it was the Preparation Day, that the bodies should not remain on the cross on the Sabbath (for that Sabbath was a high day), the Jews asked Pilate that their legs might be broken, and that they might be taken away. ³²Then the soldiers came and broke the legs of the first and of the other who was crucified with Him. ³³But when they came to Jesus and saw that He was already dead, they did not break His legs. ³⁴But one of the soldiers pierced His side with a spear, and immediately blood and water came out. ³⁵And he who has seen has testified, and his testimony is true; and he knows that he is telling the truth, so that you may believe. ³⁶For these things were done that the Scripture should be fulfilled, "Not one of His bones shall be broken." ³⁷And again another Scripture says, "They shall look on Him whom they pierced."

171. *Buried in a Borrowed Tomb*

Mk 15:42-46 ⁴²Now when evening had come, because it was the Preparation Day, that is, the day before the Sabbath, ⁴³Joseph of Arimathea, a prominent council member, who was himself waiting for the kingdom of God, coming and taking courage, went in to Pilate and asked for the body of Jesus. ⁴⁴Pilate marveled that He was already dead; and summoning the centurion, he asked him if He had been dead for some time. ⁴⁵So when he found out from the centurion, he granted the body to Joseph. ⁴⁶Then he bought fine linen, took Him down, and wrapped Him in the linen. And he laid Him in a tomb which had been hewn out of the rock, and rolled a stone against the door of the tomb.

Jn 19:39 ³⁹And Nicodemus, who at first came to

Jesus by night, also came, bringing a mixture of myrrh and aloes, about a hundred pounds.

Mk 15:47 ⁴⁷And Mary Magdalene and Mary the mother of Joses observed where He was laid.

Lk 23:56 ⁵⁶Then they returned and prepared spices and fragrant oils. And they rested on the Sabbath according to the commandment.

172. Efforts to Seal the Grave

Matt 27:62–65 ⁶²On the next day, which followed the Day of Preparation, the chief priests and Pharisees gathered together to Pilate, ⁶³saying, "Sir, we remember, while He was still alive, how that deceiver said, 'After three days I will rise.' ⁶⁴Therefore command that the tomb be made secure until the third day, lest His disciples come by night and steal Him away, and say to the people, 'He has risen from the dead.' So the last deception will be worse than the first."

⁶⁵Pilate said to them, "You have a guard; go your way, make it as secure as you know how."

After Death Appearances

173. Out of the Tomb

Matt 28:2-4 ²And behold, there was a great earthquake; for an angel of the Lord descended from heaven, and came and rolled back the stone from the door, and sat on it. ³His countenance was like lightning, and his clothing as white as snow. ⁴And the guards shook for fear of him, and became like dead men.

Jn 20:1-2 ¹Now the first day of the week Mary Magdalene went to the tomb early, while it was still dark, and saw that the stone had been taken away from the tomb. ²Then she ran and came to Simon Peter, and to the other disciple, whom Jesus loved, and said to them, "They have taken away the Lord out of the tomb, and we do not know where they have laid Him."

Mk 16:2-4 ²Very early in the morning, on the first day of the week, they came to the tomb when the sun had risen. ³And they said among themselves, "Who will roll away the stone from the door of the tomb for us?" ⁴But when they looked up, they saw that the stone had been rolled away—for it was very large.

Lk 24:3-7 ³Then they went in and did not find the body of the Lord Jesus. ⁴And it happened, as they were greatly perplexed about this, that behold, two men stood by them in shining garments. ⁵Then, as they were afraid and bowed their faces to the earth, they said to them, "Why do you seek the living among the dead? ⁶He is not here, but is risen! Remember how He spoke to you when He was still in Galilee, ⁷saying, 'The Son of Man must be delivered into the hands of sinful men, and be crucified, and the third day rise again.'"

Matt 28:6-8 ⁶"He is not here; for He is risen, as He said. Come, see the place where the Lord lay. ⁷And go quickly and tell His disciples that He is risen from the dead, and indeed He is going before you into Galilee; there you will see Him. Behold, I have told you."

⁸So they went out quickly from the tomb with fear and great joy, and ran to bring His disciples word.

Lk 24:8 ⁸And they remembered His words.

174. Peter and John Race to the Tomb

Jn 20:3-10 ³Peter therefore went out, and the other disciple, and were going to the tomb. ⁴So they both ran together, and the other disciple out-ran Peter and came to the tomb first. ⁵And he, stooping down and looking in, saw the linen cloths

lying there; yet he did not go in. ⁶Then Simon
Peter came, following him, and went into the
tomb; and he saw the linen cloths lying there, ⁷and
the handkerchief that had been around His head,
not lying with the linen cloths, but folded together
in a place by itself. ⁸Then the other disciple, who
came to the tomb first, went in also; and he saw
and believed. ⁹For as yet they did not know the
Scripture, that He must rise again from the dead.
¹⁰Then the disciples went away again to their own
homes.

175. Mary Sees the Lord

Mk 16:9 ⁹Now when He rose early on the first day
of the week, He appeared first to Mary Magdalene,
out of whom He had cast seven demons.

Jn 20:11–17 ¹¹But Mary stood outside by the
tomb weeping, and as she wept she stooped down
and looked into the tomb. ¹²And she saw two
angels in white sitting, one at the head and the
other at the feet, where the body of Jesus had lain.
¹³Then they said to her, "Woman, why are you
weeping?"

She said to them, "Because they have taken
away my Lord, and I do not know where they have
laid Him."

¹⁴Now when she had said this, she turned
around and saw Jesus standing there, and did not
know that it was Jesus. ¹⁵Jesus said to her,
"Woman, why are you weeping? Whom are you
seeking?"

She, supposing Him to be the gardener, said to Him, "Sir, if You have carried Him away, tell me where You have laid Him, and I will take Him away."

¹⁶Jesus said to her, "Mary!"

She turned and said to Him, "Rabboni!" (which is to say, Teacher).

¹⁷Jesus said to her, "Do not cling to Me, for I have not yet ascended to My Father; but go to My brethren and say to them, 'I am ascending to My Father and your Father, and to My God and your God.'"

176. The Lord Appears to Several

Matt 28:9–10 ⁹And as they went to tell His disciples, behold, Jesus met them, saying, "Rejoice!" So they came and held Him by the feet and worshiped Him. ¹⁰Then Jesus said to them, "Do not be afraid. Go and tell My brethren to go to Galilee, and there they will see Me."

Lk 24:9–11 ⁹Then they returned from the tomb and told all these things to the eleven and to all the rest. ¹⁰It was Mary Magdalene, Joanna, Mary the mother of James, and the other women with them, who told these things to the apostles. ¹¹And their words seemed to them like idle tales, and they did not believe them.

177. Lies from the Guards

Matt 28:11–15 ¹¹Now while they were going, behold, some of the guard came into the city and

~ 255 ~

reported to the chief priests all the things that had happened. [12]When they had assembled with the elders and consulted together, they gave a large sum of money to the soldiers, [13]saying, "Tell them, 'His disciples came at night and stole Him away while we slept.' [14]And if this comes to the governor's ears, we will appease him and make you secure." [15]So they took the money and did as they were instructed; and this saying is commonly reported among the Jews until this day.

178. Jesus Joins the Emmaus Travelers

Lk 24:13-32 [13]Now behold, two of them were traveling that same day to a village called Emmaus, which was seven miles from Jerusalem. [14]And they talked together of all these things which had happened. [15]So it was, while they conversed and reasoned, that Jesus Himself drew near and went with them. [16]But their eyes were restrained, so that they did not know Him.

[17]And He said to them, "What kind of conversation is this that you have with one another as you walk and are sad?"

[18]Then the one whose name was Cleopas answered and said to Him, "Are You the only stranger in Jerusalem, and have You not known the things which happened there in these days?"

[19]And He said to them, "What things?"

So they said to Him, "The things concerning Jesus of Nazareth, who was a Prophet mighty in deed and word before God and all the people, ²⁰and how the chief priests and our rulers delivered Him to be condemned to death, and crucified Him. ²¹But we were hoping that it was He who was going to redeem Israel. Indeed, besides all this, today is the third day since these things happened. ²²Yes, and certain women of our company, who arrived at the tomb early, astonished us. ²³When they did not find His body, they came saying that they had also seen a vision of angels who said He was alive. ²⁴And certain of those who were with us went to the tomb and found it just as the women had said; but Him they did not see."

²⁵Then He said to them, "O foolish ones, and slow of heart to believe in all that the prophets have spoken! ²⁶Ought not the Christ to have suffered these things and to enter into His glory?" ²⁷And beginning at Moses and all the Prophets, He expounded to them in all the Scriptures the things concerning Himself.

²⁸Then they drew near to the village where they were going, and He indicated that He would have gone farther. ²⁹But they constrained Him, saying, "Abide with us, for it is toward evening, and the day is far spent." And He went in to stay with them.

³⁰Now it came to pass, as He sat at the table with them, that He took bread, blessed and broke it, and gave it to them. ³¹Then their eyes were opened and they knew Him; and He vanished from their sight.

³²And they said to one another, "Did not our
heart burn within us while He talked with us on the road, and while He opened the Scriptures to us?"

179. Shocking News for the Disciples

Lk 24:33–35 ³³So they rose up that very hour and returned to Jerusalem, and found the eleven and those who were with them gathered together, ³⁴saying, "The Lord is risen indeed, and has appeared to Simon!" ³⁵And they told about the things that had happened on the road, and how He was known to them in the breaking of bread.

180. Jesus Appears—Thomas Believes

Lk 24:36–43 ³⁶Now as they said these things, Jesus Himself stood in the midst of them, and said to them, "Peace to you." ³⁷But they were terrified and frightened, and supposed they had seen a spirit. ³⁸And He said to them, "Why are you troubled? And why do doubts arise in your hearts? ³⁹Behold My hands and My feet, that it is I Myself. Handle Me and see, for a spirit does not have flesh and bones as you see I have."

⁴⁰When He had said this, He showed them His hands and His feet. ⁴¹But while they still did not believe for joy, and marveled, He said to them, "Have you any food here?" ⁴²So they gave Him a piece of a broiled fish and some honeycomb. ⁴³And He took it and ate in their presence.

Jn 20:20–29 ²⁰When He had said this, He showed them His hands and His side. Then the disciples were glad when they saw the Lord.

²¹So Jesus said to them again, "Peace to you! As the Father has sent Me, I also send you." ²²And when He had said this, He breathed on them, and said to them, "Receive the Holy Spirit. ²³If you forgive the sins of any, they are forgiven them; if you retain the sins of any, they are retained."

²⁴Now Thomas, called the Twin, one of the twelve, was not with them when Jesus came. ²⁵The other disciples therefore said to him, "We have seen the Lord."

So he said to them, "Unless I see in His hands the print of the nails, and put my finger into the print of the nails, and put my hand into His side, I will not believe."

²⁶And after eight days His disciples were again inside, and Thomas with them. Jesus came, the doors being shut, and stood in the midst, and said, "Peace to you!" ²⁷Then He said to Thomas, "Reach your finger here, and look at My hands; and reach your hand here, and put it into My side. Do not be unbelieving, but believing."

²⁸And Thomas answered and said to Him, "My Lord and my God!"

²⁹Jesus said to him, "Thomas, because you have seen Me, you have believed. Blessed are those who have not seen and yet have believed."

181. Breakfast with the Risen Savior

Jn 21:1-23 [1]After these things Jesus showed Himself again to the disciples at the Sea of Tiberias, and in this way He showed Himself: [2]Simon Peter, Thomas called the Twin, Nathanael of Cana in Galilee, the sons of Zebedee, and two others of His disciples were together. [3]Simon Peter said to them, "I am going fishing."

They said to him, "We are going with you also." They went out and immediately got into the boat, and that night they caught nothing. [4]But when the morning had now come, Jesus stood on the shore; yet the disciples did not know that it was Jesus. [5]Then Jesus said to them, "Children, have you any food?"

They answered Him, "No."

[6]And He said to them, "Cast the net on the right side of the boat, and you will find some." So they cast, and now they were not able to draw it in because of the multitude of fish.

[7]Therefore that disciple whom Jesus loved said to Peter, "It is the Lord!" Now when Simon Peter heard that it was the Lord, he put on his outer garment (for he had removed it), and plunged into the sea. [8]But the other disciples came in the little boat (for they were not far from land, but about two hundred cubits), dragging the net with fish. [9]Then, as soon as they had come to land, they saw a fire of coals there, and fish laid on it, and bread. [10]Jesus

said to them, "Bring some of the fish which you have just caught."

¹¹Simon Peter went up and dragged the net to land, full of large fish, one hundred and fifty-three; and although there were so many, the net was not broken. ¹²Jesus said to them, "Come and eat breakfast." Yet none of the disciples dared ask Him, "Who are You?"—knowing that it was the Lord. ¹³Jesus then came and took the bread and gave it to them, and likewise the fish.

¹⁴This is now the third time Jesus showed Himself to His disciples after He was raised from the dead.

¹⁵So when they had eaten breakfast, Jesus said to Simon Peter, "Simon, son of Jonah, do you love Me more than these?"

He said to Him, "Yes, Lord; You know that I love You."

He said to him, "Feed My lambs."

¹⁶He said to him again a second time, "Simon, son of Jonah, do you love Me?"

He said to Him, "Yes, Lord; You know that I love You."

He said to him, "Tend My sheep."

¹⁷He said to him the third time, "Simon, son of Jonah, do you love Me?" Peter was grieved because He said to him the third time, "Do you love Me?"

And he said to Him, "Lord, You know all things; You know that I love You."

Jesus said to him, "Feed My sheep. ¹⁸Most

assuredly, I say to you, when you were younger, you girded yourself and walked where you wished; but when you are old, you will stretch out your hands, and another will gird you and carry you where you do not wish." [19]This He spoke, signifying by what death he would glorify God. And when He had spoken this, He said to him, "Follow Me."

[20]Then Peter, turning around, saw the disciple whom Jesus loved following, who also had leaned on His breast at the supper, and said, "Lord, who is the one who betrays You?" [21]Peter, seeing him, said to Jesus, "But Lord, what about this man?"

[22]Jesus said to him, "If I will that he remain till I come, what is that to you? You follow Me."

[23]Then this saying went out among the brethren that this disciple would not die. Yet Jesus did not say to him that he would not die, but, "If I will that he remain till I come, what is that to you?"

182. Last Meeting with the Disciples

Matt 28:16–17 [16]Then the eleven disciples went away into Galilee, to the mountain which Jesus had appointed for them. [17]When they saw Him, they worshiped Him; but some doubted.

Lk 24:44–47 [44]Then He said to them, "These are the words which I spoke to you while I was still with you, that all things must be fulfilled which were written in the Law of Moses and the Prophets and the Psalms concerning Me." [45]And He opened their understanding, that they might comprehend the Scriptures.

⁴⁶Then He said to them, "Thus it is written, and thus it was necessary for the Christ to suffer and to rise from the dead the third day, ⁴⁷and that repentance and remission of sins should be preached in His name to all nations, beginning at Jerusalem."

Matt 28:18-20 ¹⁸And Jesus came and spoke to them, saying, "All authority has been given to Me in heaven and on earth. ¹⁹Go therefore and make disciples of all the nations, baptizing them in the name of the Father and of the Son and of the Holy Spirit, ²⁰teaching them to observe all things that I have commanded you; and lo, I am with you always, even to the end of the age." Amen.

Mk 16:16-18 ¹⁶"He who believes and is baptized will be saved; but he who does not believe will be condemned. ¹⁷And these signs will follow those who believe: In My name they will cast out demons; they will speak with new tongues; ¹⁸they will take up serpents; and if they drink anything deadly, it will by no means hurt them; they will lay hands on the sick, and they will recover."

Lk 24:49 ⁴⁹"Behold, I send the Promise of My Father upon you; but tarry in the city of Jerusalem until you are endued with power from on high."

183. The Lord Returns to the Father

Lk 24:50-53 ⁵⁰And He led them out as far as Bethany, and He lifted up His hands and blessed them. ⁵¹Now it came to pass, while He blessed them, that He was parted from them and carried up into heaven. ⁵²And they worshiped Him, and returned to Jerusalem with great joy, [53]and were continually in the temple praising and blessing God. Amen.

Mk 16:20 [20]And they went out and preached everywhere, the Lord working with them and confirming the word through the accompanying signs. Amen.

JOHN'S FINAL TESTIMONY

184. *John Has His Last Say*

Jn 20:30–31 ³⁰And truly Jesus did many other signs in the presence of His disciples, which are not written in this book; ³¹but these are written that you may believe that Jesus is the Christ, the Son of God, and that believing you may have life in His name.

Jn 1:14–17 ¹⁴And the Word became flesh and dwelt among us, and we beheld His glory, the glory as of the only begotten of the Father, full of grace and truth.

¹⁵John bore witness of Him and cried out, saying, "This was He of whom I said, 'He who comes after me is preferred before me, for He was before me.'"

¹⁶And of His fullness we have all received, and grace for grace. ¹⁷For the law was given through Moses, but grace and truth came through Jesus Christ.

Jn 21:24–25 ²⁴This is the disciple who testifies of

these things, and wrote these things, and we know that his testimony is true.

²⁵And there are also many other things that Jesus did, which if they were written one by one, I suppose that even the world itself could not contain the books that would be written. Amen.

THE LAND OF THE GOSPELS